VOICES
OF LAMENT

Reflections on Brokenness and Hope
in a World Longing for Justice

EDITED BY
NATASHA SISTRUNK ROBINSON

Revell

a division of Baker Publishing Group
Grand Rapids, Michigan

Published by Revell
a division of Baker Publishing Group
PO Box 6287, Grand Rapids, MI 49516-6287
www.revellbooks.com

Printed in the United States of America

Library of Congress Cataloging-in-Publication Data
Names: Robinson, Natasha Sistrunk, 1979– compiler.
Title: Voices of lament : reflections on brokenness and hope in a world longing for justice / Natasha Sistrunk Robinson.
Description: Grand Rapids, MI : Revell, a division of Baker Publishing Group, [2022] | Includes bibliographical references.
Identifiers: LCCN 2021061035 | ISBN 9780800740900 (cloth) | ISBN 9781493438938 (ebook)
Subjects: LCSH: Bible. Psalms, XXXVII.—Devotional literature. | Bible. Psalms, XXXVII—Criticism, interpretation, etc. | Christian women—Religious life. | Minority women—Religious life.
Classification: LCC BS1450 37th .R63 2022 | DDC 223/.206—dc23/eng/20220224
LC record available at https://lccn.loc.gov/2021061035

The author is represented by the literary agency of Credo Communications, LLC Agency.

Some names and details have been changed to protect the privacy of the individuals involved.

Patreece Lewis illustrated the internal artwork. She is the designer and artist of P. Lewis Art Collection. Find her on Instagram @plewiscollection and info@barakaology.com.

In Memoriam

Hays Jenkins, Jr.
Brother-in-law of K. A. Ellis
June 14, 1949–January 23, 2021

James Carlton Graham, Jr.
Godson to Lisa Rodriguez-Watson
May 29, 1991–January 11, 2021

Luis Flores
Grandfather to Bethany Rivera Molinar
December 23, 1931–May 23, 2021

Myrna S. Proper
Mother of Marlena Graves
May 3, 1946–June 27, 2021

Phillip Mose Berryhill
Cousin to Mariah Humphries
September 22, 1974–November 12, 2020

Pu Hwi Cho and Po Sun Cho
Grandparents-in-law of Grace P. Cho
December 22, 1929–June 8, 2020
February 5, 1934–January 6, 2021

Robert James Berryhill
Uncle to Mariah Humphries
December 8, 1932–December 6, 2020

Wilbur Moore
Brother of Kristie Anyabwile
November 13, 1957–November 6, 2020

This book was written during the COVID-19 pandemic. Some of our loved ones listed here lost their lives to it, along with millions around the world. We honor our deceased while lifting up the millions whose names may be unknown to us but are certainly known by God. We pray for all people as grief continues to move its way through our communities.

CONTENTS

FOREWORD

From first contact to the current racial climate in the United States, Women of Color have been victims of suppression and oppression. As a result, we have been long-suffering. Through the generations, our existence has been the source of disdain. Our bodies and our minds have suffered through the centuries, but despite generational suffering, we have held on to hope and belief that we are more than our oppressors' opinion of us. That belief, that faith and hope in God, has filled the following pages of stories, exegeses, essays, poetry, and liturgies.

You are about to be blessed by the faithfulness of Christian women, even when God's timing of true equity does not necessarily mirror our own. In these reflections from Women of Color, we are reminded that our current and historical cultural traditions and family legacies reject the mindset of our oppressors. Individually and collectively as diverse people groups, we are created by God exactly as we are, and we refuse to accept less.

Natasha Sistrunk Robinson has brought a collection to the forefront that shows the beauty and depth of Women of Color voices and shared experiences. This book takes us on a journey of pain and loss, admiration and respect, inspiration and hope. In the following pages we receive an in-depth view of Psalm 37, as the lived experiences and beautiful testimonies of our matriarchs and ancestors are brought to life through the historical reflections.

Many reflections in *Voices of Lament* immediately resonated with me. Some of these stories are familiar because they are a part of my story and shared history. Others of them are new, bringing knowledge and insight for the important work of bridge-building, for which I have committed my life. This is what makes *Voices of Lament* a classic work that is so important for all of us—in it, we see ourselves, and we also have the opportunity to become students of our sisters.

This book is an anthem of the power of Indigenous, Black, Asian, and Latina women, and indeed Women of Color across the world. It is a gift to each of us and a reminder that we are still here standing, fighting for justice, speaking the truth, and purposing to hope for such a time as this. Our strength and resolve have been initiated by God, inspired by our ancestors, and supported by the women who continue to influence us.

This book is for anyone who is broken, longing for justice, and trusting that "Jesus is a rock in a weary land."[1] These insights invite you to feast, fellowship, listen, and learn at the table of the marginalized. Read the powerful words of these women of faith and witness how God leads and uplifts the blameless, no matter how the systemic structures seek to weigh us down. Our cries of lament are also cries of strength and resolve as we continue on the journey of justice. For you to pursue justice, you must first have eyes to see, ears to hear, and a heart to understand injustice.

This is the work of building bridges: when we come together, willing to learn from one another, we begin to understand how we are interconnected and why we need one another. In this work, we gain strength and unity by embracing our individual and collective stories. That's the deepest gift that this book offers; may we embrace it.

To the Women of Color, I love us. Let us rejoice that *Voices of Lament* shows our love for us.

Latasha Morrison, founder of Be the Bridge
and author of *Be the Bridge*

ACKNOWLEDGMENTS

My musings began in summer 2020 and were inspired by the book of expository devotions on Psalm 119, *His Testimonies, My Heritage: Women of Color on the Word of God*. I contributed to that work, which was edited by Kristie Anyabwile. I reflected on it as I spent this unimaginable summer—which included the lingering effects of COVID-19 and the aftermath of George Floyd's murder by the state—reading through the Psalms and the book of Jeremiah.

Personally, I was nearly a year into an unexpected move, as a Black woman living in Alabama. I was lonely, isolated, and anxious. Yet God and I continued to commune together. He reminded me that he was near and concerned with my struggles. So, I thank God and my husband and daughter for persevering through such a difficult time, for cooking and eating well, for cleaning, for schooling and working virtually, for allowing long evening walks, for the days when there was art, and music, and movies, and laughter, and for not quitting when none of those things were present.

Months later, we prepared to move back to North Carolina, but our house wasn't ready. Sweet friends created a haven as my husband and I drove through Washington, DC, on my birthday and during the first insurrection of our lifetime. For nearly two months, we were houseless but not homeless, because Anne and David made their home available to us. They created a space for being with home-cooked meals and table fellowship, nature walks and geese, games, snowball fights, and opportunities to sit still by the water. It was the best place to write and edit this book, and that's mostly what I did. Thank you.

I thank God for Andrea Doering, editorial director of Revell Books, who seriously considered my vision for this project, took time to read and reflect on Psalm 37, and believed in and got behind this project from the very beginning. Throughout the process, our editor, Kelsey Bowen, was a fierce advocate and champion. I am also grateful for the editing team, proofreaders, and fact-checkers who did amazing work to ensure that we spoke the truth with integrity. Thank you, Kristin Kornoelje and Linda Washington! The entire Revell team has been a delight to work with. Thank you for centering Women of Color throughout this process, inviting and supporting Helena Brantley to join us on the journey.

I want to thank my prayer team and great community of friends who continue to undergird me and my work. My teammate, Kara, for having my back on many occasions and keeping our writing community informed and accountable.

Finally, a special thanks to the contributors: You believed and trusted God and me to deliver this classic work. You were vulnerable and gracious to share your stories. You joined me in prayer and committed to shifting the way the industry and society present our stories. You wrote, edited, and worked without complaint. There would be no book without you all. Together, we have built a community, and I pray that it is a source of support and inspiration for you going forward.

My God, I thank you for these authors, editors, advocates, organizers, organizational leaders, community builders, and pastors. I thank you for these daughters, sisters, mothers, wives, grandmothers, and friends.

I thank you for the brilliance of our poets and liturgists, and I thank you for THEEE PATREECE LEWIS, who took my heart, passion, and vision and created art before reading a single word. Sis, I believe in you and have no regrets about my decision. Your professionalism and desire to get every piece right matched my desire to honor the individuals, people groups, cultures, and legacies shared throughout the book. Without my asking, you went back to the blank page again and again because you love and care about us and our stories. May God bless you every time that you lay your pen to paper or brush to canvas.

My God, you have done it again. To you alone be praise.

INTRODUCTION

Answering the Call to Lead in the Dark

The world was on fire again, not only because a global pandemic was taking thousands of lives each day but also because there was another incident of racialized violence on a Black body in the United States of America. This time it was the knee of a police officer on George Floyd's neck for nine minutes and twenty-nine seconds. Mr. Floyd called out to his deceased Black mother before his body lay dead in the street.

There was a video that I did not initially watch, because even without it, this incident reinforced generational racialized trauma. I know the wilderness of this fight for racial justice all too well. But this time was different. This time a Black man was dead, and all over the world, cries and protests rang out in the streets.

Women of Color know about crying over our dead and making public protests. We do not turn away when our loved ones die prematurely or are murdered and crucified unjustly by the state. We are Rizpah (2 Sam. 21:1–14), who stood watch when several of her family members were murdered by the king, and Naomi, who lost her husband and her two sons (Ruth 1:3–5). We are Jochebed, Miriam, Shiprah, and Puah, who cried out and worked tirelessly to preserve the lives of their brown baby boys, who were violently under attack by the empire (Exod. 1–2:11). We are Mary looking up at the cross, and Martha, who was the first sister to cry out to Jesus, "If you had been here, my brother would not have died" (John 11:21). Whether we are heard or not, Women of Color have learned how to cry out to God in our darkest moments.

The year 2020 brought COVID-19, and I was in yet another wilderness. I thought, *God is trying to get our attention.* I was reading through the book of Jeremiah and the book of Psalms. The focus of Jeremiah is to present God's judgment to God's people because of their covenant infidelity and worldwide sin. It is a historical reflection of Israel's experience. It expresses God's faithfulness and their shared hope for the future. In the good biblical practice of corporate confession and Lamentations, I read and repented my way through the book of Jeremiah. When I came across Jeremiah chapter 9, the truth of the words from the "weeping prophet" and a call to leadership kept tugging at my heart.

Where Are the Women Leaders?

In verses 17–18, Jeremiah shares the Lord's command:

> Consider now! Call for the wailing women to come;
> > send for the most skillful of them.
> Let them come quickly
> > and wail over us
> till our eyes overflow with tears
> > and water streams from our eyelids.

These wailing women were most likely professional mourners. Notice, however, that God and Jeremiah are not calling the women emotional or insignificant. The women are not silent. They are not nice to have around. No, they call the women "skilled" because the women had learned and practiced the spiritual discipline of mourning. They are called upon to lead the community in wailing because they had been there before! They know exactly what to do when death and destruction are all around.

I believe that God's women must rise quickly now to lead us and show us all how to respond to this present darkness.

Jeremiah continues speaking directly to the women in verses 20–21:

> Now, you women, hear the word of the LORD;
>   open your ears to the words of his mouth.
> Teach your daughters how to wail;
>   teach one another a lament.
> Death has climbed in through our windows
>   and has entered our fortresses;
> it has removed the children from the streets
>   and the young men from the public squares.

The first call to the women is to listen to God. Then they are called to teach their daughters *and* their generation while they are *in* their suffering so they don't forget God's faithfulness. The women must teach their community about how God showed up to meet them *in* the dark.

I know what it feels like when the thief of death uninvitedly climbs in through my window. I am a Black woman who is the daughter of a Black man, the wife of a Black man, the sister to my mother's Black son. From poor education to mass incarceration, Black women know what it is like for our men to be taken out of the public square. When a Black man is shot in the streets, I don't care who pulled the trigger—that is cause for our wailing.

As a collective, Women of Color know that we are vulnerable, and the people whom we love are vulnerable too. We know that there is no fortress, no police, no policy, no president, no government that fights for us. God is our Strong Tower!

Women of Color know about our children being taken out on the streets. So, whether we wanted to or not, we have taught our daughters how to wail. Picture now: the unarmed thirty-two-year-old Black man Philando Castile, sitting in the driver's seat of his car after being pulled over by the police for a busted taillight. Next to him in the passenger's seat is his Black girlfriend, Diamond Reynolds, recording the aftermath of the incident on her phone via Facebook livestream because they are Black, and she knows that there is no fortress for *any* of them. The phone is her effort to show the lack of security and safety that she feels. In the back seat is their four-year-old daughter, who watched calmly as the cops shot her father multiple times at point-blank range in cold blood. After the murder, it is the Black girl—a little child—who comforts her mother, "It's okay, I'm right here with you."[1] While in the police car, she continues her plea, "Mom, please stop saying cusses and screaming because I don't want you to get shooted." And then this baby says to her Black mother, "I can keep you safe." Through her tears she cries out, "I wish this town was safer. I don't want it to be like this anymore."[2]

Whenever our men are taken out of the public square, Women of Color are the ones left behind to uphold our reputations and guard our legacies, to speak against the slander, to care for our children and grieving mothers, to figure out how bills will get paid and how we are all going to eat. We are the ones who lead our families and communities, showing them how to pick up the bloody pieces because we have been through this suffering before.

Sisters, we must encourage ourselves and each other now to unlearn the ways of the white colonizer. Our wounds are serious. May we never call for peace, when there is none (Jer. 6:14)! May we learn how to lead ourselves better and set an example for our daughters and communities about the redemptive ways of self-love, self-care, rest, and rejoicing *in* the mourning as we unapologetically pursue healing for ourselves and our communities.

As many people are being awakened to the systemic injustice of racism for the first time, the church can lead them toward righteous acts and a biblical understanding of justice that would first require humility and a willingness to sit at the feet of and learn from the women who know the ways of journeying through the dark. We have the pulse of our children and our collective communities. We have learned how to persevere through our righteous anger and lots of tears, while being ignored, abused, and silenced. We know that our children are angry and the temptation to hate is boiling over the rim so that all they want to do is yell, protest, or do anything but remain silent.

At one point during this global pandemic, I heard Pastor Charlie Dates share his concern that "we have raised up a generation that knows how to protest but doesn't know how to pray."[3] That doesn't reflect the Women of Color authors who are featured in this book. We are people of strong faith. We are also a praying and lamenting community of leaders. In the face of darkness, we stand with assurance, saying, "Because the Sovereign LORD helps [us], [we] will not be disgraced. Therefore [we] have set [our faces] like flint, and [we] know [that we] will not be put to shame" (Isa. 50:7). As leaders, we cry out to the only one that we know can help us. I am hopeful that the collective church in the United States will rise from the ashes and become the leaders that our country and our world desperately need at such a dark and difficult moment in history. And we need the leadership of Women of Color to do so.

The Call, the Culture, and the Church

I grieve this toxic environment of performance allyship and a weightless solidarity that social media has allowed our culture to create.

The urgent, knee-jerk response is always in the moment to appear relevant, "woke," or socially conscious. Real leadership and social change take long-term commitments, strategy, and planning, and the investments of resources and time. I'm looking for all people of goodwill to make a long-term commitment to justice, love, and truth-telling.

I'm looking for white people to shed their tears at home, then publicly confront the systems of oppression with their own families and personal and professional networks, and then put their money where their mouth is concerning this justice work. I'm looking for them to take ownership of and responsibility for the social, political (because it is always political), and historical problems that their people have created so that Black, Indigenous, People of Color (BIPOC) can have time and space to grieve when our lives, livelihoods, families, churches, and communities are in danger. This book is a response to "why" we *all* need to make this commitment to leadership.

In my prayers to the Lord during this season, it dawned on me that the church in the United States appears irrelevant to some and is not leading in this moment because she generally doesn't know what to do. By and large, Christian denominational, parachurch, seminary, missionary, and nonprofit leadership in the American church—like every other system and sphere of cultural influence in America—is dominated by men, most of them white. And just like in Jesus's day, although women have been faithful companions on this journey—supporting the work of ministry with our lives, resources, wisdom, and hospitality—generally we are not sitting at the tables and we are not the last ones in the rooms when critical decisions are being made that impact our lives, churches, communities, and families. Yet, we are often the ones who stand watch in the darkness, and who rise early to care for the living and the dead. Generally, we do not abandon our Savior when we do not understand or when things do not go our way. We are the faithful servants. Let us not forget that it was the women who did not scatter but followed Jesus into the darkness of the cross and the cave until the very end (Mark 15:40–41; Luke 23:55, 24:1–11, 24:22–24; John 19:25–27, 20:10–18). Indeed, Mary of Bethany was the only disciple to welcome the darkness of the cross. Being faithful to the suffering in the dark is what forever attached her name to the gospel of Jesus Christ![4]

Therefore, let us learn from the leadership of Women of Color as we answer God's call to follow him and listen to his instructions. Women of Color can lead the dirges and the ditties, the songs of justice and lament. We can lead our communities in cultivating the spiritual disciplines, as they protest and fight for justice. We can educate and teach our children and the coming generations. We can tell them about the goodness of the Lord *in* the dark. Our God has not forsaken us; he is our Strong Tower indeed!

About This Book

This book is a collaboration from Women of Color who have answered the call to leadership. Through our reflections on Psalm 37, we speak of Yahweh's faithfulness to respond to the righteous and the wicked. We are not simply sharing how God has met us individually in the darkness; we are also revealing God's faithfulness to our communities across time and throughout generations.

Psalm 37 is an acrostic poem—following the twenty-two letters of the Hebrew alphabet—that traces the themes of justice and lament. It is organized into seven strophes. "A strophe is to poetry what a paragraph is to prose. . . . [It is] a group of related lines . . . that focus on a common theme; or one idea that holds the verses in the strophe together."[5] In this book, each strophe is introduced with a poem or liturgy written by a Woman of Color that captures the theme of the strophe. The essays and prayers are presented as outlined by the Hebrew alphabet. Modeling the Psalms and the Wisdom books, these essays invite us to hear the cries of the oppressed, and grow in our empathy and human understanding, while drawing us all into deeper intimacy with God.

In the historical profiles at the end of each essay, contributors share the faithfulness of image bearers—some are Christian and some are not—who have embodied the verses' theme and have modeled this way of leadership. I invite you to sit at the feet and learn from the testimonies of these Women of Color, the elders and ancestors who have gone before us. My prayer is that these stories of brokenness shared in truth about our horrors, laments, and resilience will offer you the light of hope and love in the darkest of times. I also pray that you, too, will stand for justice and will teach your communities, your children, and the coming generations to answer this call to leadership.

PSALM 37

A Psalm of David

Do not fret because of those who are evil
    or be envious of those who do wrong;
for like the grass they will soon wither,
    like green plants they will soon die away.
Trust in the Lord and do good;
    dwell in the land and enjoy safe pasture.
Take delight in the Lord,
    and he will give you the desires of your heart.
Commit your way to the Lord;
    trust in him and he will do this:
He will make your righteous reward shine like the dawn,
    your vindication like the noonday sun.
Be still before the Lord
    and wait patiently for him;
do not fret when people succeed in their ways,
    when they carry out their wicked schemes.
Refrain from anger and turn from wrath;
    do not fret—it leads only to evil.
For those who are evil will be destroyed,
    but those who hope in the Lord will inherit the land.
A little while, and the wicked will be no more;
    though you look for them, they will not be found.
But the meek will inherit the land
    and enjoy peace and prosperity.
The wicked plot against the righteous
    and gnash their teeth at them;

but the Lord laughs at the wicked,
  for he knows their day is coming.
The wicked draw the sword
  and bend the bow
to bring down the poor and needy,
  to slay those whose ways are upright.
But their swords will pierce their own hearts,
  and their bows will be broken.
Better the little that the righteous have
  than the wealth of many wicked;
for the power of the wicked will be broken,
  but the LORD upholds the righteous.
The blameless spend their days under the LORD's care,
  and their inheritance will endure forever.
In times of disaster they will not wither;
  in days of famine they will enjoy plenty.
But the wicked will perish:
  Though the LORD's enemies are like the flowers of the field,
  they will be consumed, they will go up in smoke.
The wicked borrow and do not repay,
  but the righteous give generously;
those the LORD blesses will inherit the land,
  but those he curses will be destroyed.
The LORD makes firm the steps
  of the one who delights in him;
though he may stumble, he will not fall,
  for the LORD upholds him with his hand.
I was young and now I am old,
  yet I have never seen the righteous forsaken
  or their children begging bread.
They are always generous and lend freely;
  their children will be a blessing.
Turn from evil and do good;
  then you will dwell in the land forever.

For the LORD loves the just
	and will not forsake his faithful ones.
Wrongdoers will be completely destroyed;
	the offspring of the wicked will perish.
The righteous will inherit the land
	and dwell in it forever.
The mouths of the righteous utter wisdom,
	and their tongues speak what is just.
The law of their God is in their hearts;
	their feet do not slip.
The wicked lie in wait for the righteous,
	intent on putting them to death;
but the LORD will not leave them in the power of the wicked
	or let them be condemned when brought to trial.
Hope in the LORD
	and keep his way.
He will exalt you to inherit the land;
	when the wicked are destroyed, you will see it.
I have seen a wicked and ruthless man
	flourishing like a luxuriant native tree,
but he soon passed away and was no more;
	though I looked for him, he could not be found.
Consider the blameless, observe the upright;
	a future awaits those who seek peace.
But all sinners will be destroyed;
	there will be no future for the wicked.
The salvation of the righteous comes from the LORD;
	he is their stronghold in time of trouble.
The LORD helps them and delivers them;
	he delivers them from the wicked and saves them,
	because they take refuge in him.

לְדָוִד|
אַל־תִּתְחַר בַּמְּרֵעִים אַל־תְּקַנֵּא בְּעֹשֵׂי עַוְלָה:
כִּי כֶחָצִיר מְהֵרָה יִמָּלוּ וּכְיֶרֶק דֶּשֶׁא יִבּוֹלוּן:

בְּטַח בַּיהוָה וַעֲשֵׂה־טוֹב שְׁכָן־אֶרֶץ וּרְעֵה אֱמוּנָה:
וְהִתְעַנַּג עַל־יְהוָה וְיִתֶּן־לְךָ מִשְׁאֲלֹת לִבֶּךָ:

גּוֹל עַל־יְהוָה דַּרְכֶּךָ וּבְטַח עָלָיו וְהוּא יַעֲשֶׂה:
וְהוֹצִיא כָאוֹר צִדְקֶךָ וּמִשְׁפָּטֶךָ כַּצָּהֳרָיִם:

דּוֹם| לַיהוָה וְהִתְחוֹלֵל לוֹ
אַל־תִּתְחַר בְּמַצְלִיחַ דַּרְכּוֹ בְּאִישׁ עֹשֶׂה מְזִמּוֹת:

הֶרֶף מֵאַף וַעֲזֹב חֵמָה אַל־תִּתְחַר אַךְ־לְהָרֵעַ:
כִּי־מְרֵעִים יִכָּרֵתוּן וְקֹוֵי יְהוָה הֵמָּה יִירְשׁוּ־אָרֶץ:

וְעוֹד מְעַט וְאֵין רָשָׁע וְהִתְבּוֹנַנְתָּ עַל־מְקוֹמוֹ וְאֵינֶנּוּ:
וַעֲנָוִים יִירְשׁוּ־אָרֶץ וְהִתְעַנְּגוּ עַל־רֹב שָׁלוֹם:

זֹמֵם רָשָׁע לַצַּדִּיק וְחֹרֵק עָלָיו שִׁנָּיו:
אֲדֹנָי יִשְׂחַק־לוֹ כִּי־רָאָה כִּי־יָבֹא יוֹמוֹ:

חֶרֶב| פָּתְחוּ רְשָׁעִים וְדָרְכוּ קַשְׁתָּם לְהַפִּיל עָנִי וְאֶבְיוֹן לִטְבוֹחַ יִשְׁרֵי־דָרֶךְ:
חַרְבָּם תָּבוֹא בְלִבָּם וְקַשְּׁתוֹתָם תִּשָּׁבַרְנָה:

טוֹב־מְעַט לַצַּדִּיק מֵהֲמוֹן רְשָׁעִים רַבִּים:
כִּי זְרוֹעוֹת רְשָׁעִים תִּשָּׁבַרְנָה וְסוֹמֵךְ צַדִּיקִים יְהוָה:

יוֹדֵעַ יְהוָה יְמֵי תְמִימִם וְנַחֲלָתָם לְעוֹלָם תִּהְיֶה:
לֹא־יֵבֹשׁוּ בְּעֵת רָעָה וּבִימֵי רְעָבוֹן יִשְׂבָּעוּ:

כִּי רְשָׁעִים | יֹאבֵדוּ וְאֹיְבֵי יְהוָה
כִּיקַר כָּרִים כָּלוּ בֶעָשָׁן כָּלוּ:

לֹוֶה רָשָׁע וְלֹא יְשַׁלֵּם וְצַדִּיק חוֹנֵן וְנוֹתֵן:
כִּי מְבֹרָכָיו יִירְשׁוּ אָרֶץ וּמְקֻלָּלָיו יִכָּרֵתוּ:

מֵיְהוָה מִצְעֲדֵי־גֶבֶר כּוֹנָנוּ וְדַרְכּוֹ יֶחְפָּץ:
כִּי־יִפֹּל לֹא־יוּטָל כִּי־יְהוָה סוֹמֵךְ יָדוֹ:

נַעַר | הָיִיתִי גַּם־זָקַנְתִּי וְלֹא־רָאִיתִי צַדִּיק נֶעֱזָב וְזַרְעוֹ מְבַקֶּשׁ־לָחֶם:
כָּל־הַיּוֹם חוֹנֵן וּמַלְוֶה וְזַרְעוֹ לִבְרָכָה:

סוּר מֵרָע וַעֲשֵׂה־טוֹב וּשְׁכֹן לְעוֹלָם:
כִּי יְהוָה | אֹהֵב מִשְׁפָּט וְלֹא־יַעֲזֹב אֶת־חֲסִידָיו

לְעוֹלָם נִשְׁמָרוּ וְזֶרַע רְשָׁעִים נִכְרָת:
צַדִּיקִים יִירְשׁוּ־אָרֶץ וְיִשְׁכְּנוּ לָעַד עָלֶיהָ:

פִּי־צַדִּיק יֶהְגֶּה חָכְמָה וּלְשׁוֹנוֹ תְּדַבֵּר מִשְׁפָּט:
תּוֹרַת אֱלֹהָיו בְּלִבּוֹ לֹא תִמְעַד אֲשֻׁרָיו:

צוֹפֶה רָשָׁע לַצַּדִּיק וּמְבַקֵּשׁ לַהֲמִיתוֹ:
יְהוָה לֹא־יַעַזְבֶנּוּ בְיָדוֹ וְלֹא יַרְשִׁיעֶנּוּ בְּהִשָּׁפְטוֹ:

קַוֵּה אֶל־יְהוָה | וּשְׁמֹר דַּרְכּוֹ
וִירוֹמִמְךָ לָרֶשֶׁת אָרֶץ בְּהִכָּרֵת רְשָׁעִים תִּרְאֶה:

רָאִיתִי רָשָׁע עָרִיץ וּמִתְעָרֶה כְּאֶזְרָח רַעֲנָן׃
וַיַּעֲבֹר וְהִנֵּה אֵינֶנּוּ וָאֲבַקְשֵׁהוּ וְלֹא נִמְצָא׃

שְׁמָר־תָּם וּרְאֵה יָשָׁר כִּי־אַחֲרִית לְאִישׁ שָׁלוֹם׃
וּפֹשְׁעִים נִשְׁמְדוּ יַחְדָּו אַחֲרִית רְשָׁעִים נִכְרָתָה׃

וּתְשׁוּעַת צַדִּיקִים מֵיהוָה מָעוּזָּם בְּעֵת צָרָה׃
וַיַּעְזְרֵם יְהוָה וַיְפַלְּטֵם יְפַלְּטֵם מֵרְשָׁעִים וְיוֹשִׁיעֵם כִּי־חָסוּ בוֹ׃

STROPHE 1

PSALM 37:1–6

ONE

My Utmost Delight

A Poem by Ifueko Fex Ogbomo, Nigerian Poet

Sunrise to sunset, I pursue
Things
Necessities, naturally
For what's a belly without food?
A body without clothing?
I say, a life with no means
Is like beauty with no beholders.
And there's no making a difference
Without first making a living.
But why settle for bare necessities
If one can afford a few luxuries?
Should I strive to amass blame not greed?
But my close acquaintance with dire need
To escape the clutches of indigence
I latched on for dear life to diligence
A day without doing—
Perish the thought!
I discipline myself for I'm certain
If I run hard enough, I'll catch it:
The big break
The proverbial pot of gold
After which even with my feet up
Nothing is ever again out of arm's reach.
I seek prosperity
So I rise, morning after morning

Like a racing rodent with a cheesy crumb in sight
Chasing, *my greatest pursuit.*

Day and night, I ponder
Thoughts.
Woven from a variety of words
Reprimands parents whispered in my girlish ears
Resounding louder and louder over the years
Comments uttered by supposedly jesting peers
Cutting like double blades of sharpened shears
Sentences stated by revered voices
Sealing my fate as forever inferior
Slurs the sun-shy spit out in a moment
Staining my sun-kissed kind for all time
How is it these are the words that fill me
When they are not the words that formed me?
They're so certain, so conclusive
I forget from where they come:
Mouths that bless one minute and curse the next
That speak not what they mean or mean what they speak.
I forget these are not the words that will remain
When the heavens and the earth pass away,
Only those spoken by mouths that predate time
Printed on white pages in black or red text
Timeless truths that echo in the silence of still souls
But get lost in the traffic of troubled thoughts.
I seek identity
Yet I dwell, again and again
Upon fading words and fleeting thoughts
Denying, *my truest reality.*

Dawn 'til dusk, I desire
Fairness.
Is it really too much to ask
That karma always acts publicly
And reaping follow sowing instantly?
Shouldn't grace weigh more than gold
And doing right more than doing well?
Children shouldn't pay for their parents' choices
Status shouldn't dictate the validity of voices
Why can't judgment be based on the hue of hearts
Instead of the shade of skin or the texture of tresses?
If rewards equally matched the colors of deeds
Surely wrongdoers would never outlive weeds!
Would that no matter how badly things begin
Working out for my good is how it all ends
Alas bribe takers grow wealthy
Tale bearers grow famous
Profanity is lauded
Chastity is mocked
Injustice prances arrogantly
Unrighteousness dances brazenly
And the ears that decide never hear my own side
For their eyes have already condemned my dark hide.
I seek vindication
While I swing, back and forth
Like a pitiful pendulum, between anger and envy
Craving, *my deepest desire.*

Asleep and awake, I dream
Freedom.
What's it like to be utterly free?
A life without limitations

A mind without worries
Someone else bearing all my burdens
So I could happily live carefree
That someone would have to be special
Powerful. Truthful. Faithful.
Even if I found a friend so incredible
Ultimately, none is infallible.
Am I so blinded by mortality
I can no longer see the immortal?
God can neither lie nor fail
Why then is it so hard to trust Him?
Do I crave activity when He chooses stillness?
Seek His speaking but spurn His silence?
Perhaps I trust His power but doubt His timing
Didn't He leave His chosen people enslaved 400 years
And let His beloved son endure a bloody death?
Will He come to my rescue before it's too late
Or let me remain the ugly girl at the beautiful gate?
Alas divinity can't be weighed on humanity's scales
Hence my underestimation of His perfect love
Unrelenting. Unconditional. Utterly undeserved.
A love anyone would term "too good to be true."
Am I childlike enough to believe the incredible?
Certainly freedom cannot be found without trust.
Strong. Steadfast. Stoic.
The kind that allows a willing fall
Without net or parachute
Falling into Love
I seek liberation
But I struggle, day after day
Beneath back-breaking burdens of fears and cares
Dreaming, *my wildest fantasy.*

Moment to moment, I exist
Chasing. Denying. Craving. Dreaming.
Days grow into months
Years stretch into decades
And one question plagues me:
How am I no closer to reaching it?
My mirror tells me I grow wrinkly
My soul tells me I grow weary
Looking back it seems a wanton waste
To have pursued that which is freely given
To the birds and lilies for simply being
After what feels like a lifetime of failing
I have ended up where I should've begun:
Seeking Your face
Listening for Your voice
Meditating on Your word
Basking in Your presence
Here, in Your arms, love is unveiled
The resplendence of my righteousness, revealed:
Sure as a new dawn
Strong as the noon sun.
Here, with eyes closed, I finally see
A truth You lovingly concealed for me:
To fulfill my deepest desire I forsake my greatest pursuit
Delighting in You above all else
Liberated by Your love that embraces me just for being.
My wildest fantasy is now my truest reality
I seek no thing.
So I live
Sunrise to sunset
Day and night
Dawn 'til dusk
Asleep and awake

Soaring on wings of gratitude and ecstasy
Loving, *my utmost delight.*

Ifueko Fex Ogbomo, alias Lady InspiroLogos, is a self-employed Nigerian writer, poet, performing artist, author, and sickle cell activist. For her internationally acclaimed work in the performing arts, she was classified as an "Alien of Extraordinary Ability" and awarded United States permanent residency in 2017. She enjoys sharing the gospel through storytelling.

TWO

When the Evil Flourish

Do not fret because of those who are evil
or be envious of those who do wrong;
for like the grass they will soon wither,
like green plants they will soon die away.

Psalm 37:1–2

Marlena Graves (MDiv) is a Puerto Rican writer, adjunct professor, and PhD student living in the Toledo, Ohio, area. She has worked with migrant farm workers, asylum seekers, rural and urban poor, and in pastoral roles. She is a bylined writer for numerous venues. Her book *The Way Up Is Down: Becoming Yourself by Forgetting Yourself* won *Christianity Today*'s 2021 Spiritual Formation Award of Merit.

We expect our enemies to rise up against us and do us harm, but when fellow Christians do us dirty, commit evil against us, nail us to a cross, it's harder to recover. At least, it is for me.

Almost a decade ago, my husband, Shawn, and I both worked for a Christian organization. We had wonderful, faithful friends and loved the people we led. However, unbeknownst to us, a fundamentalist arm of the church planned a coup, a takeover of the organization. They systematically went through each department to eliminate staff they deemed persona non grata.[1] Talks and teachings concerning immigration reform, structural racism, and anti-poverty, combined with my husband and others in his department defending a friend who was falsely accused of theological drift, put us in the crosshairs of their witch hunt. They exerted great force to get rid of many of us. Suddenly, my husband's department was eliminated; my boss and even the organization's president were both gone. The new regime did whatever they could to make our lives miserable. They cleaned house.

Like Joseph's brothers, they threw us into a pit—leaving us for dead. They lied and cheated; they induced great trauma and widespread loss. Their evil antics sent many of us into financial insecurity. Indeed, their wrongdoing took a great financial, emotional, and spiritual toll on many. Shawn and I lost our best friends and our community. We have yet to recover in terms of local friendships and income.

Still, they had the gall to maintain the illusion that they were doing the Lord's work. Lying, cheating, abusing, and inducing trauma is the work of the antichrist. *If* we are going to do God's work, *then* we must use God's means to accomplish God's ends. Satan's means cannot accomplish God's work (Luke 11:14–20). The chair of the board of trustees of the organization (who resigned in protest) later contacted me with encouragement that Shawn and I had done nothing wrong—these men were just hell-bent on having their way and doing whatever it took to get it. We were all caught in the middle.

We were injured and left for dead. I lay there wounded, seething with anger while the evildoers seemingly got away scot-free. As I lay mortally injured, God played the part of the good Samaritan and met me in the pit. The Lord listened to me, sympathized, and communicated that he too knew betrayal by religious rulers and leaders. He experienced murder, literally and metaphorically, at the hands of those who stood in the name of God. Because of his own suffering and intimate understanding, he could expertly attend to my wounds. The Lord also confidently and gently clarified that eventually, if I wanted to become more like him, I would have to forgive my enemies and pray for them (Matt. 5:44). *Father, help me to forgive them, even when they know what they are doing.*

It was in this reality that I began to camp out in Psalm 37. Immediately, verses 1 and 2 stood out to me: "Do not fret because of those who are evil or be envious of those who do wrong; for like the grass they will soon wither, like green plants they will soon die away." *Really, Lord? It does not seem like they are withering or fading away. They appear to be flourishing! We're the ones fading away!*

As I meditated on Psalm 37, God began working in my heart to pray for them and to not wish them dead. I couldn't claim to follow Jesus if I nurtured hate in my heart. What's more, during that season of recovery, I realized that I, too, was capable of anger and hatred—extreme will and dislike. Catch me on my worst day, and I, too, might succumb to similar behavior. So, I repented. And repented some more. (I am still repenting.) And I also prayed for their repentance. Over time, I got to the point where I didn't want what happened to us to happen to them.

And yet, a few years later, the evildoers were dismissed by the new administration they had helped usher in. The orchestrator of it all—the one who had pulled all the strings behind the scenes—was publicly denounced and disgraced for mishandling allegations of sexual abuse at their place of employment. They were no longer in positions of power to cause further harm.

I marveled to myself and the Lord, "Look at that! I can't believe it! Those who carried out the work of evil against us are gone. Their harmful and abusive behavior caught up with them. And all this happened in the land of the living?" After reading Psalm 37:1–2, I figured that all things would be made right in God's eternal kingdom, not here and not now. I was wrong! At times, we are blessed to "see the goodness of the LORD in the land of the living" (Ps. 27:13).

Unfortunately, their downfall didn't change our situation. What was done was done. The consequences of their actions remain to this day. But I know beyond a shadow of a doubt from this example, and many others, that God is true to his Word. Indeed, I am not to worry. Do not fret over evildoers. They will reap what they sow and eventually fade away. My responsibility is to ask for the Spirit of God to help me love my enemies and pray for them, lest I, too, be consumed. I must not fuel worry, anger, bitterness, or hatred—or else I will become just like them.

Lord, help me to believe that you are in the process of making all things new right now. Reorient my mind so that I might gaze at your face instead of worrying, becoming bitter, or cultivating hatred in my heart. You are good, true, and just. Cultivate peace within me. You tell us vengeance belongs to you—not us. Help me to trust in your good judgment and timing. Amen.

Saint Teresa of Avila (1515–82)

Reforming the Church

I am biracial. From my mother's side, my lineage is a mix of Spaniard and the Taino Indians of Puerto Rico. Teresa of Avila, a Spanish mystic of Jewish descent and a canonized saint within the Roman Catholic Church, is an incredible woman to highlight because I've noticed that several Spaniards contributed to the spiritual formation and renewal of Roman Catholicism. Teresa was born in Avila, Spain, in 1515 and died in Alba, Spain, in 1582. When she was twenty years old, she became a Carmelite nun at the Monastery of the Incarnation in Avila and devoted her life to God. At one point, she became ill with malaria and fell into a coma after having seizures. Teresa's suffering drove her to depend on God. And perhaps it is because of this dependence produced by suffering that she had several personal (what some call "mystical") experiences with God. She sought to reform the Carmelite Order of the Roman Catholic Church.

We need not trip over the phrase *Christian mystic*. A Christian mystic believes in the tenets of historic Christianity and in a personal relationship with God. The mystic uses the ancient spiritual practices of meditation on Scripture, prayer, fasting, silence, solitude, community, giving alms, and many others to cultivate this personal relationship. To some extent, all of us are mystics. The spiritual disciplines we have in Protestantism have their roots in the Eastern Orthodox and Roman Catholic Churches—once the same church until the split in 1054.

In 1970, Teresa was named the first woman doctor, or official teacher, of the Roman Catholic Church. At the time, she took her place among Saint Augustine and thirty other men.[2] To be considered a doctor of the Roman Catholic Church, one must be canonized a saint and be of "eminent learning, heroic sanctity and unquestioned renown."[3]

In addition to practicing spiritual disciplines and becoming a doctor of the church, Teresa of Avila was always reforming herself and in doing so, she played a prominent role in the renewal of the Roman Catholic Church even after her death. She helped renew the discipline of prayer and other spiritual disciplines mentioned above within the Carmelite Order. She started new convents. But she had her share of opponents and detractors. Although she was a younger contemporary of Martin Luther, she remained within the Roman Catholic Church. In fact, she never dreamed of leaving the church. It is true that she had heard about groups such as Luther's, but she considered them heretical.[4] Perhaps we can say Teresa chose to remain and reform from within her sphere of influence. That is a path that many choose today. Teresa was an ordinary, yet extraordinary, woman of faith and reform during her time. Her influence continues today. She is widely known for two books: *The Way of Perfection* and *Interior Castle*. I believe it is extremely important to know our roots so as not to cut ourselves off at our roots. And in some small way, I continue in her footsteps of reforming myself and thereby reforming the American church.

THREE

Blessings in Brokenness

Trust in the LORD and do good.
> Then you will live safely in the land and prosper.
Take delight in the LORD,
> and he will give you your heart's desires.

Psalm 37:3–4 NLT

Tarah-Lynn Saint-Elien is a multi-hyphenated millennial who inspires women through her *Cosmopolitan UK* nominated brand, Adorned in Armor, and *Dressed for Battle* podcast. The *Teen Vogue* It Girl turned fashion writer was crowned Miss Black New Jersey and earned her master's from Syracuse University. The Haitian American beauty queen released her first book, *Claim Your Crown*, and *Love Letter from the King* and has been featured on CBN, the *Haitian Times*, and the YouVersion Bible app.

The energetic crooning of Christian singer-songwriter Ron Kenoly blasted through the speakers of my father's rental. He would play a mix of Kenoly's tracks, Haitian Creole albums, and Messianic Jewish worship music during our road trips.

Driving from New Jersey to Georgia during the summers of my early teenage years are some of my fondest memories. My siblings and I would sit excitedly, pestering our parents in anticipation of our arrival at our cousins' house. We'd begin our trip around 3:00 a.m. and would fall asleep, wake up and sing, fall asleep, wake up and dance, fall asleep, wake up and eat until we reached our destination.

I always woke up at the part where Kenoly sang about how God turned his mourning into dancing (Ps. 30:11). Because of his new-found joy, he couldn't stay silent. Lightly bopping my head, eyes closed with a small smile dancing on my lips, I hummed along. The trumpet tickled my ears. The flutes, drums, and other instruments I couldn't pinpoint played out a great celebration. As I leaned on the glass window, not even a night sky without stars could dim the light in my eyes.

But sometimes after a long ride, you feel a crick in your neck from resting your head on the window for hours. Joy doesn't feel like it's found in the morning when the sun's rays beam against your closed eyelids, rudely interrupting your rest with blinding views of red-orange. My eyes would dart open to find our rental pulled over to the side of the road and my mother shifting around in her seat, groaning with pain. There were many pit stops along the way, until the road trips stopped all together.

What a Girl Wants

When my mother suddenly fell ill and had to quit her nursing job, I was six years old, my brother five, my sister four, and my youngest sister only a year. Doctors diagnosed her with avascular necrosis, but all my siblings and I could understand was that "Mommy can't walk anymore," that "Mommy is in pain," and that "Mommy is in the hospital again."

Although my mother has undergone seven unsuccessful surgeries in less than ten years, her doctors still want to operate. After several near-death experiences, however, my mother continues to refuse any additional surgeries. All she wants is to watch her kids grow up—that's what she tells everyone. It's what she asks of God, and he has continually granted her request, sometimes from the view in our home, sometimes from her hospital room.

My Haitian immigrant parents ensured we had the best childhoods they could offer. Their love protected me, provided a sense of comfort and safety, so I did not think deeply about what I wanted. Desire was something my parents couldn't give. They also couldn't change a reality—particularly my mother's declining health—that was outside of their control. The psalmist encourages us to trust in the Lord, delight in him, and do good, and God will grant us the desires of our hearts. At the time, my unspoken desire was for my mother's healing; all I wanted was to have her healthy and home with our family. I have witnessed my mother trust and delight in the Lord and "do good," yet the desire for her healing has not been answered.

A Daughter's Desire

I was the child who ran out of daycare and into the street to grab hold of my mother's legs to keep her from leaving me. I was the fiercely protective middle schooler, glaring at anyone who would dare stare too long at a young mother limping with a walker and children trailing behind her. I was the college kid who always made time to speak to her mother every day while on campus. I was all this, and yet what I desired then I didn't speak of much. Even in a prayer-filled home, I thought, *This is just the way things are.*

Until enough was enough. I kept calling home right before spring break of my freshman year of college, but I couldn't reach my mother. I texted my sibling group chat to see if anyone had talked to Mom. We all tried to act like we weren't worried, but we knew something was wrong. We later discovered that our mom had been admitted into the hospital for heart palpitations, so I made plans to visit her in the hospital once I got home from campus.

Sneaking into her hospital room, my family waited for her to awaken, and when her eyes finally fluttered open, she smiled at us but began speaking random words. She recognized her children but couldn't remember our names. I quickly left the room, trying to hide my tears. That was the first time I ever cried about my mother's condition.

What now? I thought. *Hasn't she suffered enough?* I was infuriated with God.

My father explained to the nurses, "Something is wrong with my wife," and we left the hospital because visiting hours were way past over. While we were on our way home, my mother called my cell, promising me that she remembered my name, that she didn't know what was wrong but that she loved us all. I put my phone on speaker when she began reciting our names by our birth order: Tarah-Lynn, Mitchielsen, Medgina, Shermine. We later discovered what had caused the confusion. My vibrant mother had had a stroke in her sleep.

At this point, my mother was struggling physically and mentally. Right after the stroke, she had to write out what she wanted to say. Even today, she often strains to remember certain words or to finish her sentences. Her eloquent speech is sometimes sprinkled with stuttering. She sleeps irregularly due to the pain yet fights to stay up in order to pray.

Throughout the years, several unrelated issues have plagued her body. And physical therapy hasn't helped. Despite her health challenges, the numerous hospital bills, and the lack of relief via medication, she speaks truth with her lips and with her life—the "joy of the LORD is my strength" (Neh. 8:10). Our family across the globe—both extended and nuclear—look to her as our rock and joy.

When God Doesn't Heal

My own life has been a journey of realizing what I really feel. In the moments I think God has let me down, I am reminded of his character. God is good not because of the good he does for me. He is good because that is his nature, period. When we experience God as our Father who knows best, we learn to lay aside our understanding and pick up the freedom of letting him have his way in our lives. In our Job experiences, it is possible to still believe God is working things out for those who love him (Rom. 8:28), no matter how it looks or how long it takes. Even when it hurts, I will still believe in who God says he is. There is no other option for me and my house: we will serve the Lord (Josh. 24:15)!

Music reminds my family of God's goodness. My father is always humming, and one can hear my mom singing at the top of her lungs. She goes from singing her favorite *louange*[1] songs as she lies in bed to creating her own silly lyrics as she encourages herself to make a family dinner. You can find my siblings having their own concerts with headphones on their ears or observe all of us laughing through harmonization.

And still, there are times we bolt out of rooms after hearing a huge thud rattle our home late at night and find our mother on the floor. There are times when we are running with buckets of warm water sloshing to and fro as we hurry to soak her feet before her cramps get worse. There have been times when our words fail us and our prayers are replaced with silence as she is carried away from our home by ambulances.

But we continue to delight. Through my mother's testimony, I've learned to bless God for who he is, even when the healing doesn't come.

This lesson has been a difficult one to learn in one's youth. I've spent most of my teen years accepting things as they were. Suffering has been my mother's teacher. To a lesser extent, suffering has also been mine. Now, as I journey into womanhood, I am learning to believe that my mother will be healed. What I have gained on this journey is an intimacy, both with her and with God. I write my books by her bedside, and she teaches me patience. I've now learned how lamenting and trusting in the Lord grant me the freedom to express myself.

The intimacy of knowing that the loving God is near to us means that we don't have to be afraid to ask God questions when we don't understand. We can throw our anger at him, knowing he can take it. He won't push us away. It means that blessings and brokenness can occupy the same space.

> **Father, we take the blame off you.**

Even with pain in my mom's body, she dances. With words escaping her mind, she still sings.

Father, we take the blame off you. Forgive us when we're fed up and reject your presence. When we do not understand, may we keep in mind that you are the God of answers. Your hand still heals, and you are the Father who knows best. Thank you, for your glory shines brightest in suffering. In constant affliction, may we pour out our love to you to get us through. Father, thank you for freeing us to sing and dance in the only place we find peace: your presence. In Jesus's name. Amen.

Emma Jeanne Achille (1934–)

A Search for the Queen of Haitian Gospel

The internet is littered with articles arguing Haiti's alleged pact with the devil, but if you dig deeper, you may come across stories of the powerful women who helped establish Haiti as the first independent Black nation. There was Victoria Montou, the warrior woman who commanded her own Indigenous army and trained Haiti's founding father, Jean-Jacques Dessalines. There was Marie Claire Heureuse Félicité Bonheur, "the first Red Cross,"[2] who, as legend has it, was so beautiful that when she rode out to battle, the French paused their cannons as she cared for the fallen.

In my own search, I ventured into the kingdom of Haiti, "which existed as a sort of Wakanda of the Western Hemisphere from 1811 to 1820."[3] Needless to say, I was enthralled coming across our Catholic nobility: Marie-Louise Coidavid, the first queen of Haiti and the first Black Caribbean queen, and her daughters, princesses Améthyste and Athénaïre. I was rejoicing inwardly until I came across disheartening resources highlighting the erasure of our Afro-Caribbean aristocracy.[4]

I then transported my search from online to word-of-mouth, for our Western thought and education have socially conditioned us to devalue the power, legitimacy, and history of oral transmission.[5] With a blank screen in front of me and my mother lying by my right side, I turned to her and asked if she had *any* recollection of *any* Christian woman who made an impact in Haitian history. She was on the phone with my pastor, so we directed the question to him as well.

"Do you remember the lady who sang *levanjil*[6] hymns in Haiti?" my mother asked.

"Emma!" my pastor exclaimed after a long pause.

"Yes, Achille! Emma Achille," my mother said, nudging me. Excited, I turned to Google and there she was: the queen of Haitian gospel.

Older generations remember the voice of Emma Achille. She delighted in singing praises to the Lord from a young age. She championed the cause of Christ in a nation constantly barricaded by hard times and devoted over sixty years of her life to evangelical worship.[7] Achille traveled, ministered, and trusted in the Lord to bring about opportunities for his glory, and he did so in Haiti and in the United States. The queen won the hearts of her people with her velvety voice and at the age of eighty-eight represents a pillar of strength.

We can thank Achille for what Creole YouTube is today—filled with Haitian artists belting their hearts out for the glory of God. Achille's testimony, ministry, and musicianship are a reminder of the importance of keeping our oral traditions and writing them down to pass along to the next generation, all the while revealing the power of telling our own stories.

As of the writing of this article, Achille faces health challenges as a result of a stroke and is wheelchair bound in an assisted living facility. I pray the Haitian diaspora has the opportunity to pay greater tribute to this iconic woman!

FOUR

Roll Upon the Lord

Commit your way to the LORD;
   trust in him and he will do this:
He will make your righteous reward shine like the dawn,
   your vindication like the noonday sun.

Psalm 37:5–6

Sandra Maria Van Opstal, daughter of Colombian and Argentine immigrants, is the founder of Chasing Justice. She is an author, pastor, and activist reimagining the intersection of faith and justice. Her work centers contemplative activism under the mentorship of the global church, for the mobilizing of the next generation of leaders. She holds a master of divinity from Trinity Evangelical Divinity School. Her most recent books include *The Next Worship: Glorifying God in a Diverse World* and *Forty Days on Being an Enneagram Eight.*

My thoughts are not your thoughts, neither are your ways my ways,' declares the LORD. 'As the heavens are higher than the earth, so are my ways higher than your ways and my thoughts than your thoughts'" (Isa. 55:8–9). God knows the way. Trusting God is difficult to do on our best days and in good circumstances, so how do we learn to commit our way to God when the world seems to be disintegrating and life's realities are leaving us with compounded pain? How do we trust when we are jobless, spouseless, or childless? How do we commit to God when the injustice in the world has us questioning the character of its Creator?

My journey, like so many of ours, began with watching my parents and extended Latina community. The Brown church has developed a theology of suffering that has taught us to hold on to hope and joy. Unlike a theology of the powerful that deprives the people of God of the healing and deliverance they need, a theology from the margins understands that trusting in God has nothing to do with material circumstances. This devotion to God through suffering is a gift to God's body. Affection for God, even when things are difficult, is not an ignoring of the present pain; it is living in light of a promise. In communities that have been terrorized and persecuted for their race or ethnicity, trust is present. In communities where children have been ripped from parents and sold or fostered to the "churchgoing" citizens, trust is present. In communities where we've had to confront rage and depression from having our humanity assaulted, trust is present.

> Affection for God, even when things are difficult, is not an ignoring of the present pain; it is living in light of a promise.

In the same fashion as the psalmist, these difficult events that happen in life move us through three experiences we face as human beings in relation to God: orientation, disorientation, and reorientation. These stages that Old Testament scholar and theologian Walter Brueggemann proposes are present in a majority of the psalms. The thoughts and experiences of the psalmist move from declaration (orientation) through lament (disorientation) into thanksgiving (reorientation).[1] My formation was oriented around a God who is with us when we suffer, not a God who kept us from suffering. I was oriented to love a God who would provide in the midst of poverty, so I didn't see wealth as a reward of any kind.

What were you oriented around, and how disoriented did you become as you confronted the poverty in your own heart and the injustice of this world? What did it take, or will it take, to reorient you?

You see, each of us is formed in a particular location, by a distinct community. That formative experience deeply impacts what it means for us to commit to God, and whether we trust God to make our righteousness seen.

Psalm 37 is a communal psalm proposed for singing within the context of corporate worship. The grammar and historical context of this passage confirm that the audience of this psalm is a people, not a person. This might be a point of reframing for those whose reference for this passage is a wall decoration, a "you go, girl" greeting card, or a self-help book. Taken out of context, this passage reads like a spiritual platitude for a person who needs a pep talk. That distorts the Scripture and misses the point entirely, since the song was gifted by the psalmist to his community to remind them of God's character. Rightfully clarifying that this psalm uses communal worship to reflect the promise of God's presence within a collective society that is experiencing violence impacts the interpretation and weight of the verses.

We can better interpret these verses as *"YOU ALL commit YOUR COLLECTIVE way to the* Lord. *YOU ALL trust in the* Lord. *He will make YOUR COLLECTIVE righteousness known."* This is not about God making our individual or selfish plans succeed. This is a word of promise to God's people that if—even in the face of evil—we commit our lifestyles to the Lord, he will guard the collective witness of his people. We can be sure that the justice of our cause will shine!

In this first section of the psalm (from verses 1 to 7), we are given a list of commands in the imperative Hebrew form. The imperatives are bookended with the command to "trust in the LORD," which occurs in verses 3 and 5. We are exhorted to trust in the Lord (v. 3), do good (v. 3), delight (v. 4), commit our way (v. 5), and trust in him (v. 5). In between the two commands to trust God, we find specific ways to live into that reality by doing good, delighting in God, and committing our ways to him. The Hebrew understanding of *belief* was not merely intellectual or conceptual. In a holistic culture, it implied that you believed with your whole being, which included your intention, affection, and actions. It was a way of ordering and understanding life beyond your mind or heart into your behavior. To have faith, to believe, to trust in God meant that you ordered your life around God. The psalmist's invitation, therefore, echoes this holistic approach. We are invited to trust God in action by doing good, in affection by delighting, and in intention by committing our lifestyles. This way of viewing *trust* is the context of these verses.

This way of loving God is evident in the core prayer of the Hebrew people. This prayer is called the Shema: שְׁמַע in Hebrew or as translated, "hear." The prayer that is prayed daily says, "Hear, O Israel: The LORD our God, the LORD is one. Love the LORD your God with all your heart and with all your soul and with all your strength" (Deut. 6:4–5). The Hebrew idea of *heart* is where you understand life. You think and feel in your heart. It also contains your affections and desires because it is the center where all parts of human existence connect. Your *soul* literally means your throat. It describes what goes in and comes out of your body. It is what makes you a living, breathing, physical being. And the final part of "you" that is commanded to love God is your *strength*. As an adverb, *strength* means "very good"; as a noun, it is to love God with your "very muchness."[2] Love is orienting your life around God in such a way that it includes your intellect, emotions, and actions. We love God with our whole self.

The command to the people of God who have been impacted by historical, collective evil is to commit their way to a lifestyle of devotion. They are to entrust to the Lord, or literally in the Hebrew to "roll upon" the Lord, the anxiety, cares, and fear they face in the context of real danger. God's people can do this because God, Emmanuel, is with them. The Lord will bring their right or just cause from obscurity into the full light of the noontime sun. This is a word of encouragement to a group of people who feel like they've had a collective butt whupping in their sociopolitical reality. To those who are hurting and hopeless, God says, "YOU ALL commit YOUR COLLECTIVE way to the LORD. YOU ALL trust in the LORD. He will make YOUR COLLECTIVE righteousness known."

This is a whole word for God's people today, but particularly for those of us who continue chasing justice together while it seems like the wicked are winning. This is a word for us as we watch our communities struggle under policies and practices that dehumanize us while diversity initiatives tokenize us. This is a word for us as we watch the testimony of the church in the United States become an impotent witness to the next generation with each news cycle. It's as if too many leaders within institutional religion are complicit with the empire of the United States. Local communities all around the world are bravely committing to the Lord and trusting in God's ability to make their righteousness seen in the light of day. They may not be in the denominational newsletters or the podcasts, but they are faithful. Likewise, in our personal participation and faithful witness, we should hold on to the promise that God is trustworthy. We are called to orient our lives around God, knowing that God accomplishes the work of justice through God's own Spirit and in God's own time.

This psalm has carried me through many seasons of life. As a young, single woman in my early thirties, I wanted to be married, but seemingly there were no prospects in sight. A decade earlier, I'd made a commitment to God to break off an unhealthy relationship with a man I really adored, which meant I was leaving university man-less. I had no idea that I was entering a dating drought. I thought that God was going to give me the desires of my heart for trusting in him. Although my personal desires were not being met, I continually witnessed the liberating power of Jesus and his call to justice. Once I became a married woman, it took us six years and a miscarriage before my husband and I were able to bring our baby home. I was giving my vocational energy to planting churches, finishing seminary, writing books, and mobilizing for justice through the church as we committed ourselves in the context of community to keep doing good and delighting in God no matter our personal circumstances.

If I'm honest, I am tempted to give up on birthing promises in an infected womb or what seems like the barrenness of the church to produce life. I am frustrated by a drought of true worship. As a reconciler and advocate of biblical justice, I want to see the American church liberated from the idolatry of individual safety, success, and comfort. So I commit my way to the Lord, being faithful in my family, faithful as a neighbor, faithful to my local congregation, faithful in my finances, and faithful to the truth of living a life oriented toward God. Because I come from a communal people group, I understand that we ALL need each other, so it is humbling and hurtful when too many leaders in the North American church do not affirm this need or fight for my people. Yet, I trust God's righteous reward and vindication. It's hard to continually trust, but it is so worth it.

Lord, we are sorry that we have limited your promises to self-help sticky notes on our mirrors. We grieve that what you mean for communal encouragement we have turned into an individualistic exercise that not only distorts your Word but also robs us of the richness that is found in the communal journey and witness of the gospel. Forgive us. Fill us with the courage to seek good and hate evil. Fill us with the strength to make daily decisions oriented around your justice and love. Fill us with the hope we need to continue to delight in you and be faithful to your ways so that others will see that you are making all things new.

Mother Mary Teresa
(Anjezë Gonxhe Bojaxhiu) (1910–97)

A Lifestyle of Faithfulness

Anjezë Gonxhe Bojaxhiu, also known as Mother Teresa, is known for being a nun who took a vow of poverty and spent much of her life living among, working with, and advocating for the poor. She loved those who others thought of as disposable. In 1950, Teresa founded the Missionaries of Charity, which has thousands of nuns and is active in hundreds of countries. The sisters care for orphans, provide education, feed the hungry, and care for the sick (particularly those with HIV/AIDS, leprosy, and tuberculosis). Like many other orders, the sisters take vows of chastity, poverty, and obedience, and they covenant to devote their lives in free service to the earth's poorest citizens.

As a Latina woman, I am drawn to Mother Teresa as a historical figure more than to women from my own community. While I have been spiritually formed by so many brilliant theologians, leaders, and activists from within the Brown church, my formative years have deeply shaped my theology. I was a girl whose childhood was spent worshiping in a Catholic parish with my *abuela*,[3] and nuns—Mother Teresa and the Missionaries of Charity, in particular—were heroic figures to me. As an Enneagram Eight, which Teresa was as well, I am drawn to her fierce commitment to do justice, love mercy, and walk humbly with God (Mic. 6:8).

I remember one summer I had the honor of working alongside the sisters in Mokattam, just outside Cairo, Egypt, in a community of garbage collectors. As we cared for beautiful children who were disabled and orphaned, I remember feeling it was such an ordinary task. We washed dishes, hung laundry, and held children. Being faithful in the small tasks that were frustrating to repeat kept the community going. This was the summer I became aware of Mother Teresa's quotation "God does not require that we be successful, only that we be faithful." In that context, in the hot desert air filled with pig feces and fermenting garbage, I stood on the roof-deck of the monastery where we stayed and asked God to give me the wisdom to live a life of faithfulness. A year later, I prayed the same prayer with my spouse on that same roof-deck and made commitments about time, finances, and overall lifestyle.

Mother Teresa was awarded the Nobel Peace Prize in 1979 "for her work for bringing help to suffering humanity."[4] During her acceptance speech, she said, "And through this award and through all of us gathered here together, we are wanting to proclaim the good news to the poor that God loves them, that we love them, that they are somebody to us, that they too have been created by the same loving hand of God, to love and to be loved. Our poor people are great people, are very lovable people, they don't need our pity and sympathy, they need our understanding love. They need our respect; they need that we treat them with dignity."[5]

Mother Teresa wanted to influence; she had something to say. She saw distorted narratives and she wanted to help us reimagine. The way in which she influenced, however, was through her commitments to the poor and a life of simplicity and service. She used her words to accentuate her deeds. Mother Teresa's message was often piercing to those who felt challenged by her focus on the vulnerable and disenfranchised, including the unborn. Her words were an encouragement and a challenge, and her lifestyle forced people to consider their personal life choices. This powerful act of committing her way to the Lord got her into a lot of trouble, but she continued to persevere and trust that God would make her righteous lifestyle and message known.

From the author: Mother Teresa is one of the most important figures, if not the most important figure, for many Latinos. Though she was of European descent, her people, the Albanians, have been massacred by Serbian armies since the early 1900s through the present day. Albanians have been refugees, experienced genocide, and been a traumatized people group, much like those of us who hold practices of lament.

STROPHE 2

PSALM 37:7–11

FIVE

Anger, I Will Not Tame Her

A Poem by Tasha Jun, Korean American Storyteller

Anger,
I will not tame her
I will tend to her instead
My hands are not tied
They are busy with the work of love
My mouth will not stay muted
It speaks prophecy and poetry
My mind is not empty
No, it remembers

Anger,
I will not shush her
I will listen to her instead
My ears are not closed
They are open to the sound of suffering
My heart will not stay hard
It is soft like soil wet with the tears of a thousand clouds
My body will not stay rigid
It welcomes the wails of my ancestors:
Comfort women, forbidden comfort
Haenyeo,[1] who know
The dark depths of the sea
How it feels to be silent
Swimming down
Unafraid of the pressure
Proud of holding their breath to feed a hungry nation

Anger,
She tells me the sad stories and sins
She carries the weight of war and unjust systems
She wields the power of thunder, oceans, rivers, and rain
She is fire burning with the question "How long?"
She is something like courage
She roots our connected long-suffering
She reminds us who we wait for

To refrain from her rage,
I must first let her speak

Anger,
Show me your tears and your sorrow
Sing me your cries of not-yet
Your songs of the oppressed
Teach me how to hope for a better tomorrow
and resign to the things I was never meant to burn down

I will wait with you like my 엄마 and her 어머니² before her
I will look ahead for our God
A burning bush
A hot coal
A fire pit to stand beside while the rooster crows again
and we remember how much we need a Savior
who knows
who feels
who sees
who loves
who is worthy to bring justice
who doesn't delay

Anger,
I will hope with you
for a wide space of mended land

It's just ahead
A little while longer now

Anger,
tell me about the places that are still broken
I will sit still with you
while you become a glowing ember of warmth and light
I will seek what's still unseen
let my heart be searched clean
I will bring you to a place to lie down
and rest,
Anger.

Tasha Jun is a Korean American writer, storyteller, and poet. She grew up in a multicultural, biracial family in cities all over the world. She is married with three kids. She writes about faith, ethnic identity, belonging, family, and finding beauty and shalom. Her work has appeared in numerous online and print publications, devotionals, and Bible studies.

SIX

My Ancestors' Perseverance, My Voice to Carry

> Be still before the LORD
> and wait patiently for him;
> do not fret when people succeed in their ways,
> when they carry out their wicked schemes.
>
> Psalm 37:7

Ruth Buffalo is a citizen of the Mandan, Hidatsa, and Arikara Nation and originally from Mandaree, North Dakota. She is married to Brian, and they have two sons and two daughters. She is an educator, public health professional, and politician. Ruth is serving a four-year term as a state house representative in the North Dakota legislature, representing District 27. She is a women's peacemaker fellow and founder of Local Innovative Leadership Initiative.

I was born in 1978, the year the American Indian Religious Freedom Act was passed. I grew up in a disciplined household, raised by a single mother. I believe that I am led and guided through my values and the legacy of my grandparents and ancestors. My upbringing was filled with hard work, laughter, outdoors, and faith in our Creator. I am a citizen of the Mandan, Hidatsa, and Arikara—known as the Three Affiliated Tribes.

Many of our cultural teachings and values parallel Christianity. This is often misunderstood and has contributed to historical and intergenerational trauma. Yet, I know that it is God who knew me and gave me purpose before placing me in my mother's womb. I carry my late maternal grandmother Ruth's English name and her traditional Hidatsa name, "Woman Appears." My lineage comes from beautiful, noble, and courageous people.

Surviving Wicked Schemes

Psalm 37:7 says, "Do not fret when people succeed in their ways, when they carry out their wicked schemes." This verse speaks to me as I reflect on the Native Nations in the United States. Our country has policies and systems that were put in place to decimate the Native American population completely.[1] As we know, legality does not always equal justice. We were forced from our ancestral land, our children were removed from their homes and placed in boarding schools, and laws restricted our spiritual lifeways—all designed to diminish over 570 Tribal Nations. Yet, we survived and persevered, and we are still here, thriving.

One "well-meaning" policy, the Pick-Sloan Act of 1944, was intended to create water resources for the Missouri River Basin. The result included the displacement of my people from the land they had inhabited for generations. The flooding of 94 percent of the agricultural lands of the Hidatsa forced many to relocate to other parts of the United States. My family chose to stay on the rough, barren grazelands to which they were relocated and where we currently reside—present-day North Dakota.

Wickedness takes many forms. Perhaps the most devastating system established to achieve cultural genocide of the Native Nations was the boarding or industrial school system. Developed by Brigadier

General Richard Henry Pratt, the motto and practice was to "kill the Indian and save the man."[2] The goal was to assimilate Native children into Eurocentric practices and appearances. This was put into motion by removing cultural practices, changing their dress, cutting their hair, banning their first language, and separating them from others who were of the same Tribal Nation. Children suffered trauma from being in solitude and from being abused—physically, emotionally, mentally, and sexually.[3]

Generational trauma from these acts continues today. I am reminded daily of the perseverance, stillness, and patience of entire Tribal Nations who continue to move forward despite the challenges they have endured. They did not give up when the white man carried out his wicked schemes. Therefore, we cannot give up. It is not an option.

Raising My Voice over the Wicked

My mother was an example of enduring strength. When I was four years old, I witnessed a priest from a nearby church self-righteously tell her that we should go back to where we came from. We left that church abruptly, but my mother's faith was strong. She did not fret when evil people succeeded in their wicked ways. We continued to attend a different Catholic church west of Mandaree, on the reservation where our Hidatsa culture and traditions were integrated into every aspect: from the altar and songs to midnight mass at Christmastime. This integration built a strong sense of faith among our community. It showed me that I could maintain both my culture and my belief in God.

Growing up, I attended a nearby boarding school because of a lack of academic options and transportation limitations on my reservation. Uniforms were required, and one day before school started, I took my large load of books to my locker. There I was reprimanded by our principal, a nun. She stopped me and pulled me into the classroom next to her office. As she pulled up my skirt, she made a remark about her perception of my appearance. She yanked my shirt down through the inside of my skirt. I was shocked as I stood there with my arms outstretched, experiencing the same abuse and humiliation other Native children have lived through. When she was finished, I returned to my dorm room and cried on my bed from the sheer embarrassment and horror of the experience.

After I told my mother what had happened, we immediately went to see the principal. I was shocked again, standing beside my mother, as I heard this authority figure deny her actions. I was raised to believe there are good and bad people, and this early experience in life showed me that people in authority can make mistakes. I decided then that I would become a better leader and continue to raise my voice against the wicked. Instead of becoming bitter, I advocate for my family and for people I do not know. I have learned how to "be still before the LORD and wait patiently for him" (Ps. 37:7). I trust the Creator that a righteous path will be cleared for me.

Being connected to the Creator God means that our spiritual journey must include stillness and patience, especially in the face of injustice. For it is God who "make[s our] righteousness shine like the dawn, [and our] vindication like the noonday sun" (Ps. 37:6). This vindication is revealed in the poetic justice of God allowing me to become a public servant in the political arena. I am a servant of God, so I do not consider myself a politician. As God's agent, I am in the belly of the beast within the state legislature. At times the environment is hostile, and I remind myself daily of who I am, where I come from, and why I serve.

Carrying My Ancestors with Me

Just like those of my ancestors before me, my patience and purpose are tested. The 2021 legislative session proved to be challenging as I faced opposition with every bill I introduced, but I know where I need to be at this time in history. So I trust God through all the challenges placed before me, including being an elected official.

Each day on the house floor, the session opens with a prayer followed by the Pledge of Allegiance. From the moment I was sworn in, I have honored my Hidatsa culture and tradition by sitting during the prayer, as women do, while the men stand. This is done not out of protest or submission but out of the respect men have for women within our culture and tradition. We are the life givers, and they are our protectors.

It is my honor to bring the legacy and traditions of my ancestors into the public sphere and to pass on their teachings to the next generation. My faith in humanity is continually renewed by the future generations. They are what breathes life into me. So, carrying my voice for them includes honoring my ancestors, my culture, and my heritage even in the way that I dress.

One day a young lady came to the state capitol during a session to show support for a particular bill. She saw me wearing a skirt similar to hers, a ribbon skirt. She asked if I was heading to "that hearing." I replied, "Yes." She laughed and said, "I am going to follow you. You look like someone I can trust." After the hearing, I walked with a group of Native American women through the halls of the capitol, and the same young lady shared her amazement at how tall I am. She said that she wants to be the next Ruth Buffalo. Those words made my heart soar.

Inspiring this young woman reminds me that I do not have to fret even when I struggle and endure hardships. God is faithful to redeem and restore what has been broken. There was a time when

I was traumatized while wearing a skirt. Today, I proudly wear my ribbon skirt to stay in prayer and to show the strength and perseverance of my ancestors and my voice.

Maaxubahaxidea, mi igaa, biki gidashadzi, maciigiraac.[4] *Creator God, please hear my prayer, for I am pitiful. Thank you for the many blessings you provide for us each day. Please continue to give peace and strength to the mourners, the brokenhearted, the lonely, the homeless, those struggling with addiction. Maaxubahaxidea, mi igaa, biki gidashadzi, maciigiraac.*

Ruth Rabbithead Buffalo Bolman (1916–76)

A Still and Quiet Life before the Lord

My grandmother Ruth, after whom I am named, was a very spiritual woman and the glue to her family. She weathered many storms throughout her life, but her faith in our Creator God carried her through. She built faith and community around her family. My middle name is the namesake of her good friend Anna, who worked at the Mandaree Clinic. Another one of her friends was my godmother, who was present throughout my life. In the same way that her friends cared for me, my grandmother served her community. She was the mother of eleven children, three of whom died at an early age.

My grandmother and grandfather were happily married, and they had a lovely partnership. My grandmother was known for her beautiful star quilts and beadwork. My grandfather designed the beadwork that she beaded. After the flooding of Elbowoods led to massive relocations of tribal communities, my grandfather ran into challenges finding work off the reservation, so my grandmother helped bring in income with her sewing and beading skills. She helped keep the family together, because that's what women do. Within her family, she instilled a love for each other and a love for the Creator God.

She was a strong believer, and as a result named two of her daughters Faith and Hope. She was an active member in the Ladies Auxiliary and later served in the capacity of a community health representative for Mandaree. To this day, people share with me stories of how my grandmother helped them. Many remember her providing several families with rides to the doctor. My grandma had many friends in the community who were present in her children's and grandchildren's lives long after she was gone.

One year before I was born, my grandmother died at sixty years old from breast cancer. My grandfather passed away six months later, many say from a broken heart. Together, they left a rich legacy of faith and family.

In 2012, not long after we lost my baby sister to a drunk driver, my eldest brother told me, "The only way we are going to make it through these tough times is through faith and family." I believe this is true; faith and family sustained both of my grandparents when they attended boarding schools. Faith and family have sustained all of us through adversity.

Although she is not a historical figure in the traditional sense of the word, I lift up my grandmother Ruth as a representative of all the Native Tribe women and ancestors whose stories have been lost or ignored. I carry her name and her legacy, and I believe that her prayers are still guiding and protecting our family, her community, and our people to this day. She never gave up, she had hope and faith in the future, and no matter what curveballs life threw at her, she trusted in her Creator God.

SEVEN

Pursuing Justice May Start with Anger

Let go of anger and leave rage behind!
Don't get upset—it will only lead to evil.

Psalm 37:8 CEB

Kathy Khang is a Korean American writer, speaker, and yoga teacher based in the north suburbs of Chicago. She is the author of *Raise Your Voice: Why We Stay Silent and How to Speak Up* and serves on the board of Christians for Social Action.

My being can cause discomfort.

I stood up to face my colleague and matched his posture, his volume. I took up space and pointed at him, speaking loudly over the din of the restaurant. While he was raising the volume of his voice, standing up and gesturing toward me to make his point, people paused, but the way I remembered the moment was that everything stopped when I stood up to speak my mind and matched his posture and raised my voice.

I was angry. Not in the moment, but in the moments and hours following, I was angry. Angry that my behavior, and not my male colleague's behavior, was singled out as unprofessional, aggressive, and concerning. Angry that not one but several colleagues approached me privately about my behavior, and I got angrier when I later confirmed no one had done the same with my male colleague. Angry that once again I felt unheard and unseen despite several people approaching me to voice their concerns with how they interpreted my behavior. In the moment, I wasn't angry. I was trying to get my point across, raising my voice and volume, standing up and physically taking up space, believing we were living in a world that saw me and my colleague as both fully human with permission to express ourselves. I wasn't angry until I was told I couldn't look angry, let alone be angry.

I spent the rest of the evening with two other women who knew intimately what I had felt, and their company and counsel reminded me that it was wise and important to name my emotions but not let that moment of anger be the driving force moving forward.

Anger is a misunderstood emotion and reaction. Growing up as a Korean American girl in the Midwest, I experienced a lot of emotional suppression. In my home, there was always a level of keeping the peace, and that also applied at church. You couldn't be angry at church. You couldn't be angry with God. Somewhere along the line it just became translated into "anger is a sin." At school, you couldn't be angry at the bullies because they would threaten you more, and when you were one of the first children of color in the school district, the goal wasn't to stick out but to become invisible. My physical appearance made that impossible, so to survive I put my head down, studied harder than everyone else, and drew attention away from what made me different. In the case of bullying, the playground advice was "don't be a snitch" and simply tolerate the pain. My invisibility was reinforced on so many levels.

The psalmist gives readers verse after verse of emotions. Anger, despair, surrender, joy, peace, and confusion. But what happens when we express these emotions? What are we to make of these emotions, and what is the psalmist suggesting we are supposed to *do* with our emotions? How are we supposed to feel and act when despair or anger or even joy take over our hearts and minds? What does that look like and how or why should we leave that part of ourselves behind?

The psalmist informs us that anger, when not released, can change us; it can change our behavior and motives from desiring and chasing after justice to performing evil acts of personal revenge and spite. The psalmist reminds us that a life in the pursuit of God's kingdom shouldn't overwhelm our souls or cause us to act with evil, selfish revenge. Instead, it frees us from the weight of anger.

Seeking Pleasure from the Comfort of Women

Becoming aware of "comfort women" weighed me down with anger. I didn't learn about them until my late twenties, in part because there were no Korean history classes to take and also because it wasn't until the early 1990s when stories from surviving comfort women gained public attention.

Comfort women most often were not consenting adults, and they certainly did not exist in comfort. They are the thousands of girls and young women who were coerced, trafficked, and forced into sexual slavery by the Japanese Imperial Army from the 1930s until the end of World War II. The United Nations estimates that two hundred thousand girls and women were forced into the Imperial Army's sexual slavery program.[1] The girls were from Korea, China, the Philippines, and other countries under Japanese colonization and occupation. For decades, Japan denied the comfort women's testimony, claiming they had volunteered—were willing participants—or were already prostitutes. The term *comfort women* stems from the role they allegedly played in "bringing comfort" to the men who served in the Japanese Imperial Army.

Even as I write the words *comfort women*, I can feel the anger well up inside me. These were not women of comfort, nor was the sexual slavery they were subjected to a matter of someone else's actual need, let alone comfort. These women, many of whom were girls, were raped by men seeking physical pleasure at the expense and dehumanization of girls and young women. How, then, do these women not live angry? And how do we not get angry learning about their plight? When I think about the abuse of these women, that is the moment when the psalmist's admonition to "let go of anger and leave rage behind" doesn't sit well with my soul. That is the moment we enter into someone else's pain, and maybe our own, and see how anger can be righteous and compel us to desire and seek out justice and a new ending.

As I read their stories and began my own journey of identifying and healing from trauma, I started to better understand the psalmist's admonishment. This verse, when isolated, can be easily taken out of context from the poetry and songs of a book that explores how our emotions can imprison *and* free us. Does anger take a different form for those who claim to follow Christ? Yes. I say it must. Succumb to the isolation of emotion from our life's values as Christ followers and the anger can transform into evil. Who hasn't had a momentary thought of seeking revenge or lashing out in anger with words or actions aimed only to hurt? We must remember that anger is not inherently evil. The psalmist isn't telling us not to feel. Rather, he is telling us not to let our emotions get the best of our imaginations and our actions.

Kim Hak-Sun was the first comfort woman to come forward publicly. She had not forgiven the men, but she also did not let anger have the final word. Her public testimony gave others the courage to raise their voices, thereby forming both a community of survivors and a community of supporters and allies who protested weekly as they continued to seek a formal apology from the Japanese government and an acknowledgment of the injustices they had endured.

I believe that the full invitation of the psalmist is to name our anger, to invite community into our healing and desires for justice, and then to leave anger behind as we lean into the promises of God, who is the God of comfort and giver of peace that surpasses all our understanding (Phil. 4:7).

God, Creator of our embodied souls, thank you for not being afraid or dismissive of our emotions. Thank you for giving us the imagination to chase justice without allowing the anger of injustice to swallow us whole. Amen.

Kim Hak-Sun (1924–97)

Women and the Art That Truly Comforts

After sharing her story publicly in 1991, Kim Hak-Sun filed a class-action lawsuit against the Japanese government, which at that time denied their responsibility and claimed the women had not been forced into sex slavery. "When I was young, I could not say what I wanted to say because I was so afraid that I would get killed (by the Japanese). For crying out loud! How could I live without saying a word? So that's why I decided to share my story before I die. Even if it meant risking my life. There may be no one else but me to tell this story. That's why." Even in her last days, Kim Hak-Sun continued this righteous pursuit to tell the truth about the rapes and injustices that comfort women experienced.[2]

After Kim's courageous move to speak out, hundreds of other women were moved to add their stories to the public record despite the continued doubt some historians and government officials tried to cast, as well as the public shame they would experience recounting stories of their own rapes. Their collective courage moved others into action as well. Public protests convened weekly on the streets of Korean cities. Another public response was the *Statue of Peace*, also known as the Comfort Women Statue—a memorial and public work of protest art—erected in 2011.

Artists Kim Seo-kyung and Kim Eun-sung explained in an interview with CNN that originally a memorial stone was planned but the Japanese government publicly criticized the effort. Instead of voicing their anger at the Japanese government, the artists created the *Statue of Peace*, which depicts a young Korean girl sitting alone but next to an empty chair, an invitation to move from being observers looking at the girl and contemplating her trauma to sit alongside survivors as advocates and allies.[3] Similar statues continue to be erected in cities with significant Korean populations, once again reminding us of how art, whether the poetry and song of the psalmist or public protest sculptures like the *Statue of Peace*, helps tell a story and allows the artist and the audience to name their emotions and trauma, and eventually heal.

EIGHT

Displacement and Belonging

For those who are evil will be destroyed,
　　but those who hope in the LORD will inherit
　　　　the land.
A little while, and the wicked will be no more;
　　though you look for them, they will not be
　　　　found.
But the meek will inherit the land
　　and enjoy peace and prosperity.

Psalm 37:9–11

Kat Armas is a Cuban American writer and podcaster from Miami, Florida. She is the author of *Abuelita Faith: What Women in the Margins Teach Us about Wisdom, Persistence, and Strength* and the host of *The Protagonistas* podcast. Her work sits at the intersection of race, ethnicity, gender, spirituality, and Scripture.

I've always felt a deep connection to the story of the Israelites. Like theirs, my story is one that is shaped by exile, displacement, and a longing to be replenished in the land of my ancestors.

My *abuela* arrived in the US nearly fifty years ago, leaving her home country, Cuba, at the height of political unrest that displaced hundreds of thousands of Cubans from the island. While

Abuela has lived most of her life in the United States, her spirit still longs for the familiar sounds, smells, and scenery of her homeland. *"Mis huesos serán enterrados en una tierra que no es mía* [My bones will be buried in a land not my own]," she tells me.

I find displacement and longing an interesting phenomenon. The realities of my family's displacement and consequent sentiments of not belonging imprint in the body and in the spirit, and both are passed on from generation to generation. The desire to create an affirming space for ourselves in this foreign land can be seen when you walk through the streets of my hometown, Miami, where thousands of Cubans settled after the revolution. First-, second-, and even third-generation Cubans have re-created our heritage in the city, ensuring that our foods, culture, and customs aren't forgotten. Although we are displaced, the connection to and the love of our island are too strong to ignore. Collectively, our hearts beat to the rhythm of the *congas* from our island. We're here, but we're still there. This duplicity is rooted in my DNA and pulses through my veins as powerful as Cuban *café*[1] at three in the afternoon.

As I was growing up, *Abuela* always kept the memory of Cuba alive. My most vivid childhood memories are of us strolling through her garden, picking fruit for our afternoon snack. It was during these times when she came most alive, recalling stories and details of her island—the palm trees that offered respite from the warm Caribbean sun; the plants that provided our family's nourishment; and the animals that befriended her as a young child. While we dug our hands in the ground and felt the soil between our fingertips, she spoke of Cuba as if it were still hers, as if it were ours.

When my family left Cuba in the 1960s, they never imagined they wouldn't return. Many who fled at that time buried their valuables in their backyards, keeping maps drawn on napkins hidden in their pockets, hoping to resurrect them the moment their feet once again touched the soil that birthed them. Many, including my own *familia*, still wait with patient longing for that moment, even though most know it will never come. For this reason, my whole life I've experienced nostalgia for a land I've never lived on. While this can feel strange, the Bible reminds me that it isn't unfamiliar. As I've learned from the Israelites, *the land lives within us*—in our bodies, in our spirits, and in our memories.

God's People in Exile

There are certain prevalent themes carried throughout Scripture, like love, justice, and care for one's neighbor. Similarly, one theme that prevails is that of journeying. The Bible tells narratives of people journeying to one land or leaving another, with tales and depictions of deportation and displacement at the center. As such, even the consistent themes of justice and care flow in and through narratives of journeying.

Wrapped up in displacement and deportation is the notion of exile. Much of the Hebrew Bible relates to it: the pain and suffering of forced migration, the consequent challenges of resettlement, and the overall crisis of exile[2]—which includes lack of safety, hardship on the body, and violence, among other things. In the Bible, exile can be understood as a physical uprooting from one's homeland as well as a general distance from God.[3] Even when it is long past, exile continues to shape the identity and self-understanding of those who experience it.

Similarly, exile is what forms the identity of the Cuban diaspora. It names who we are communally and historically as a people, in the same way that the Israelites' exile to Babylon— after the destruction of Jerusalem and the temple in 586 BCE—marked the end of the Jews' political sovereignty and the interruption of the Davidic monarchy.

Those who survived the Babylonian exile were forced to negotiate a new sense of belonging and find fresh meaning in life as a collective people of God. This process can be traced throughout Scripture and even today within the cacophony of voices expressing generational trauma, lament, ambivalence, and courage, as well as an uncertainty and searching for personal, religious, and political identity.[4]

There's a famous psalm in Scripture that expresses this pain vividly. Psalm 137:1–6 details the yearnings of the Jews during the Babylonian exile, and it reveals an ache of nostalgia, distress, and desire:

> By the rivers of Babylon we sat and wept
>   when we remembered Zion.
> There on the poplars
>   we hung our harps,
> for there our captors asked us for songs,
>   our tormentors demanded songs of joy;
>   they said, "Sing us one of the songs of Zion!"
>
> How can we sing the songs of the Lord
>   while in a foreign land?
> If I forget you, Jerusalem,
>   may my right hand forget its skill.
> May my tongue cling to the roof of my mouth
>   if I do not remember you,
> if I do not consider Jerusalem
>   my highest joy.

This psalm is both deeply political and deeply religious. It is a vivid communal lament that details the heart's cry of many who have been uprooted from all that made their lives meaningful.[5] Like the psalmist, those who have experienced exile are profoundly affected by the notion of remembrance: we are determined to never forget our land. *Let me forget my right hand if I forget you, Cuba.* To cling to one's memory is to cling to identity and to attempt to keep alive a world that might otherwise vanish from our memories.[6]

For the Israelites, to remember Zion was to affirm who they were in a foreign place, to remember the land of their ancestors and every-thing God had done for them. Some say that those who had been political, social, and religious leaders of Judah were now subject to labor—many forced to work as diggers of irrigation canals.[7] The evil and the wicked in Psalm 37 bring to mind the captors—those who humiliated God's people by asking them for songs of entertainment despite their anguish. Exiles sit by the rivers of their host country, reflecting on their inability to sing God's songs in a foreign land. How could they?

Body and Land

Throughout time, land and people have been closely intercon-nected. Lands have symbolized peoples across the globe, as well as the cultural narratives that make up who they are.[8] Thus, the struggle of earth and land is intimately connected with the struggle of body and soul. For this reason, Scripture reveals that both body and land are sacred. The Spirit of God resides in the bodies of be-lievers and, from the beginning of creation until now, works in and among the land.

For the people of God, land offers security, prosperity, and peace, as we read in Psalm 37. Since the first image bearers inhabited the garden of Eden, humans have worked and grounded themselves in the land (Gen. 2:4–7, 15). At the beginning of creation, human beings were commissioned to watch over the earth and all created things, to look after them, and to receive nourishment from them (1:26–31). The connection between God and God's creation—the land and all its creatures—in the Genesis narrative is sacred, and according to God, "very good." Just as Adam and Eve learned, distance from the land leads to anguish, anxiety, and uncertainty. On the contrary, throughout Scripture, being restored to one's land equates to being blessed by God—to being cared for and looked after by the divine.

This relationship among creation continues to play out throughout history—across time and across communities. If sojourners came across a people group while on their journey, it always meant they'd come across the land the people were connected to and the animals that were an extension of their family. This divine sense of creaturely connection was part of God's original plan in the garden and is why displacement and exile can often feel unbearable and unnatural.

Resurrection

Spending time with *Abuela* in her garden felt holy. Additionally, pulling weeds and planting were the sacred actions of reconnection with the land and with God when the weight of exile felt too heavy. Even now, when I long for a garden of Eden reality—when the injustices that plague our world feel unbearable—I find myself going back to those holy moments with *Abuela* when our fingernails were covered in dirt. While participating in God's redemption plan, flourishing, and resurrecting our heritage and culture in a new place, we humbly remembered our humanness and the temporary state of our earthly exile. *We are soil and to soil we will return* (Gen. 3:19).

Resurrection is coming—a time when we will return to the land as it was designed, when the meek will inherit it and enjoy peace and prosperity. Until then, we continue to uproot and to plant, to tear down and to build up (Eccles. 3:2–3), and to fight for the dignity and care of creation and all created things on earth as it is in heaven.

God of all creation, those who you created from dirt are privileged to bear your image. We recognize the sacredness of all that you have made—of the land, its people, and animal-kin. Remind us of our earthliness and restore the relationship between all created things so that we may be whole. Amen.

Rigoberta Menchú (1959–)

A Sacred Fight for Freedom

Tucked away in the mountains of Guatemala in El Quiche is a small village called Chimel, made up of seventeen families of Mayan people. The first Indian and first Latin American woman to receive a Nobel Peace Prize was born in this small community. Her name is Rigoberta Menchú.

Growing up, Menchú had a deep connection with the land and with her people. At a young age, she joined the Catholic Church and began advocating for social reform for the Indigenous community from which she came. Menchú's activism took center stage during her teenage years at the height of the Guatemalan civil war. During this time, called the *guerra sucia*, "the dirty war," the Guatemalan army tortured, devastated, and attempted to displace the Indigenous people of the Quiche region, prompting Menchú and her family to organize and fight back.

Eventually, Menchú's father, brother, and mother were captured and murdered by the government, forcing Menchú into exile, where she joined international efforts to make the Guatemalan government cease its brutal attacks against Indigenous peasants.

Menchú spoke publicly about the plight of the Mayan people in Guatemala while in exile, eventually publishing her autobiography, titled *I, Rigoberta Menchú*, which catapulted the civil war into global headlines. Her struggle for justice eventually earned her a Nobel Peace Prize in 1992.

Menchú's activism speaks to the liberative and liberating Word of God, as she has been vocal about her love for the Bible and how it taught her people to defend themselves against oppressors. Through her study of Scripture and her commitment to her land and her people, Menchú fought for a garden of Eden reality, even while in exile.

STROPHE 3

PSALM 37:12–17

NINE

Lying in Weight

A Poem by Medgina Saint-Elien, Haitian American Poet

The world was never my oyster, so I made it a bed.
I seek comfort within thick sheets.

To cushion the weight of nighttime.
It's a twisted pattern; the fabric blanketed over my
    body.

Eyes open; I am as tired as the day before.
The chips and nicks along the structure of the bed's
    frame mark my days of waiting.

And you in your opulent silk sheets, and feathery
    pillows,
Elevate high above the tattered cotton mattress that
    yearns to suffocate me.

Some count sheep, others cloak themselves in
    bloodstained wool,
Preying on the cries of wingless birds.

I was taught to ignore the monster under the bed,
How it torments the dreamers who dare to touch the stars.

In the stillness of the dark, I allow myself to drift to
    where You promised me
While the beast beneath sharpens its claws.

I glide my fingers over ridges of the shell's open mouth,
Palms memorize the cool polish.

An iridescent glow from the center sends diamond-
    shaped rays to the sky,
The false rainbow a sign of danger to come.

To my left, footprints in the sand mirror those who
    sought greed over justice.
Conchs beckon me forward, to slide over its slopes and
    gills.

I've seen what sows when pristine hands pry the jewel
    from its throne,
How fast it will clamp shut, gnash teeth on ankles and
    cling without give.

> *I hear You whisper "Look out,"*
> *And step away from the snare.*

The pearl is not as lustrous up close, bruised pink and blue
Tempted to bleed scarlet.

Foragers gather around the oyster,
Knives gripped to gut riches from its core.

The ocean crashes, foams, groaning at waves of violence
I hide beneath the shadow of the sun.

But You have them placed in position—kneeling and
    backs exposed.
The mouth shuts, collapsing on the schemes of the
    wicked.

On my right, I lie in a king-sized fortress.
The satin sheets pool us together rather than apart;

> *I roll up my mat,*
> *Carrying more than enough on my shoulders.*

Medgina Saint-Elien is a writer and creative who is called to high-light the elephant in the room throughout her work. This Haitian American poet is a Fulbright Scholar and an emerging voice of direction in the media industry. She redefines beauty at Byrdie Beauty, Snapchat, and beyond to amplify the stories of Women of Color.

TEN

When Will Their Day Come?

The wicked plot against the righteous
and gnash their teeth at them;
but the Lord laughs at the wicked,
for he knows their day is coming.

Psalm 37:12–13

Bethany Rivera Molinar is a *fronteriza* Chicana living and
working in El Paso, Texas. She is the executive director of
Ciudad Nueva Community Outreach and serves on the
board of the Christian Community Development Association.
Bethany is passionate about faith-based community development and worshiping God with mind, body, and spirit.

When I was a child, my parents told me that I would
grind my teeth at night. They said the sound was so
loud they could hear it from their bedroom. Since I was asleep,
I was never conscious to hear myself do it. I used to wonder
about the mechanics of it all—how could my teeth make such
loud noises? Whenever I tried to consciously grind my teeth, I
could never make an audible sound. Later, I learned that there
are many reasons why people grind their teeth at night. Sometimes it is a result of an overbite or an underbite. Sometimes it
is due to stress or anxiety.

While I am not sure what caused my own teeth grinding, the cause of the grinding described in Psalm 37:12 is clear. The gnashing of the wicked's teeth is a bodily manifestation of their intense hatred and anger toward the righteous. Their hatred is so encompassing that it contorts their countenances. Their anger is aggressive, focused, and strategic.

There are several examples of gnashing of teeth in the Old and New Testaments. One instance can be found in the book of Acts. Stephen, the church's first martyr, was the victim of a public lynching (Acts 6:8–8:2). Like the psalmist, Stephen believed in a good and just God whose gospel was bigger than the religious powers believed and whose presence could not be confined to a physical space. The gospel that Stephen believed in was proclaimed through the miraculous acts he performed, the ways he served, the sacrifices he made, and the words he preached. But this same gospel angered some of the religious leaders. To silence Stephen, his accusers planned and executed a campaign against him. Then they, along with the angry mob they emboldened, seized Stephen, brought him before the high priests, and accused him of blasphemy.

Stephen was ultimately given a chance to speak. With the humble and submissive countenance of his Savior, Stephen proclaimed that the gospel was bigger than what was preached and practiced in the temple. By recalling to the religious leaders *their own immigrant story*, he made it clear that God is not confined to any physical space. He spoke of Abraham, who was called by God to leave his home country. And Joseph, who was trafficked by his own brothers and taken to a foreign land. He spoke of the people of Israel, who were enslaved and mistreated in Egypt, many who did not live to see the liberating promises made to their ancestors. He spoke of Moses, who wandered from a palace in Egypt to the desert of Midian, where God met him in the wilderness, giving him the charge to free the enslaved Israelites.

Stephen continued, speaking of God's people in the wilderness, who did not have a homeland for forty years. He cited these examples of God going before his people as they traveled through foreign lands to show them that God was always with them, no matter the place, for "the Most High does not live in houses made by human hands" (Acts 7:48). Their own ancestorial story testified to this! Finally, Stephen turned to his accusers and accused *them* of committing grievous acts against God. They were enraged! The Scripture says,

> When the members of the Sanhedrin heard this, they were furious and gnashed their teeth at him. But Stephen, full of the Holy Spirit, looked up to heaven and saw the glory of God, and Jesus standing at the right hand of God. "Look," he said, "I see heaven open and the Son of Man standing at the right hand of God." (7:54–56)

Stephen did not see "the day come" for his accusers, as the psalmist speaks about in Psalm 37:13. Rather, to those witnessing this scene, it looked like *Stephen's* day had come. But God stood with Stephen even as he was brutally murdered. Though he did not live to see it, Stephen's message spread among Jews and Gentiles. In this way, God laughed at their wicked intentions to shut down the proclamation of the gospel. Their plans were indeed futile and frustrated. Even if Stephen did not get to see the end of the story, we did. We do every day. Ultimately, Christianity continues to spread throughout much of the world as followers of Jesus migrate. From Stephen's day until now, it bears a good news message that comes with power to transform people and entire communities. The day of the wicked has already come, indeed.

In the US/Mexico borderlands, it is not hard to identify the wicked, because the wicked have blatantly sought our destruction. At the border, we know and feel their wrath. We see the gnashing of their teeth. Our people have suffered greatly from their horrific plans. The rhetoric spoken from national platforms by powerful people has leached into our skin like poison: "When Mexico sends their people, they don't send their best. . . . They're sending people that have lots of problems, and they're bringing those problems with us. They're bringing drugs. They're bringing crime. They're rapists. . . ."[1]

The wicked calculated, and their strategic policies have caused chaos, confusion, grief, and trauma to image bearers of God. God sees when children are being separated from their families.[2] God sees the woman whose infant was ripped from her breast as she nursed.[3] God sees humans being stored like cattle under a bridge in the deadly heat.[4] God sees asylum seekers purposely stranded at bus stations by US Customs and Border Protection on Christmas Eve[5] to make our border city appear chaotic.

The dissension the wicked have stirred up has caused violent acts that terrorize our community. Right after a "hate-filled, anti-immigration manifesto appeared online," twenty-three people were executed by a white supremacist who bought into the lies that the wicked in positions of power told in order to stir up dissension against us.[6]

We see the wicked gnashing their teeth, their faces contorted by their hatred of us. We are overwhelmed by their plans for our destruction. Grief upon grief and trauma upon trauma have made it hard to believe that their plans will be laughable, or that they will not accomplish their ultimate purpose. It can be hard to see that their day is surely coming.

But God was with Stephen, even in his brutal death. And God was with Abraham and Sarah; Moses and Zipporah; the Virgin Mary and Joseph; and countless more in their displacement. And God stands with us too. God walks with us *now*. And we are compelled to trust that God is good and just. We press in and hold on with faith that the day of the wicked *will* come.

How do we do this? By living. Our very bodies and our continued survival as a people testify to a just and good God who will not allow the plans of the wicked to destroy us. We worship and lament together through our collective prayers, the lighting of candles and incense, and the music of mariachis[7] leading us in song over the loss of our precious sisters and brothers at the hands of the wicked.[8] We practice being and togetherness by sitting with our *comadres y compadres*,[9] holding hands, weeping and crying out for God to incline his ears toward us in our deep grief.

We prophesy that the plans of empire are for naught by banding together and refusing to leave our asylum-seeking brothers and sisters stranded at a bus stop. We place our faith in a *good* God who loves and cares deeply for vulnerable people marginalized by empire. We receive our asylum-seeking brothers and sisters as we would receive Christ (Matt. 25:34–40), even if it means splitting the bag of beans in a sparse pantry so that no one goes to bed with an empty stomach.

We choose to walk in faith when we help our neighbors navigate their pain, giving them space to process and mourn. Together as a community, we identify the lies we have been told by empire. And we replace those lies with the truth that God deeply loves us and delights in who God has created us to be. We remind Brown children and adults alike that their presence in our community is a blessing and that they are altogether valued and needed to help our communities thrive.

Stephen died before he saw the gospel spread throughout the world, so we understand that we may not live to see our prayers answered. But we still trust that the kind and merciful God we serve hears our prayers and responds. God has never abandoned his people. The wicked may gnash their teeth, but our continued existence declares that their plans for our destruction will fail.

Good and just God, we cry out to you. Hear our prayers. Hear our cries. See our suffering. Walk with us. Suffer with us. Be the light of our countenances. And fulfill your promises to deliver us from the hands of the wicked. Amen.

Carmelita Torres (1900?–Unknown)

Her Spirit Still Lives

Not much is known about Carmelita Torres.[10] We don't know exactly when she was born or when she died, nor do we know most of her life's story. We do know that as a transborder Mexicana, she spent her life on both sides of the US/Mexico border, as she made her home in Juarez, Chihuahua, and her living cleaning houses in El Paso, Texas. We also know that when she was subjected to degrading and dangerous policy at the hands of US immigration officials and a racist mayor, she said, "No more."

In 1915, Tom Lea Jr. was elected mayor of El Paso. Lea sensational-ized typhus (a disease spread by lice) to justify his racist agenda of terror in the name of hygiene. This resulted in the razing of 130-plus adobe homes inhabited by poor people of Mexican descent and led to the fiery deaths of twenty-seven prisoners who were subjected to kerosene baths.

Lea enacted a policy in 1917 that forced Mexican citizens trav-eling across the international border into El Paso to go through a dangerous and humiliating disinfection process to cross the US border. Mexicans were divided into groups by sex and doused with kerosene as their clothing was steamed and sprayed with toxic pes-ticides. They were inspected for lice, and any suspicion of lice led to their hair being shaved. Mexicans were required to repeat this dangerous process every eight days for entry into El Paso.[11] There were also reports that immigration officials secretly took photos of the women when they were naked and posted them in local bars.[12]

When she was a teenager, Carmelita traveled across the border daily by trolley for work. One morning as her trolley approached the bathhouses on the US side of the bridge, she realized she had had enough and refused to step into the bathhouses. Carmelita's boldness, courage, and anger prompted other women present with her to resist. Together they stepped off the trolley and refused to leave the bridge. Within hours, two hundred women joined her, and like Jesus at the temple, they disrupted the business of the day because that inhumane business was inherently wicked. The women lay on the bridge and threw rocks and bottles at vehicles attempting to pass. By day's end, thousands joined Carmelita and the women, shutting down the border for two days.

Carmelita was arrested, and the rest of her story is lost to history. Some of the men who participated in the riots were executed. The policy of forcing Mexican border crossers to take these baths continued into the 1960s, along with the use of increasingly dangerous chemicals like Zyklon B and DDT.[13] Much like in Stephen's story, it seemed like the plans of the wicked would prevail.

Yet, the story and fight of this righteous woman live on. Carmelita was courageous. She stood up to her oppressors and said, "No more!" She declared her own humanity and that of her people by standing up to the wicked powers that be. Today on the border, we remember her. We carry her spirit as we continue to fight against degrading and inhumane policies that seek our people's destruction.

ELEVEN

Bending the Bow of Peace

> The wicked draw the sword
> and bend the bow
> to bring down the poor and needy,
> to slay those whose ways are upright.
> But their swords will pierce their own hearts,
> and their bows will be broken.
>
> Psalm 37:14–15

Jenny Yang is the senior vice president of Advocacy and Policy at World Relief, where she provides oversight for all advocacy initiatives and policy positions for the organization and leads the organization's public relations efforts. She is a Korean American leader who has worked over a decade in refugee protection, immigration policy, and human rights. Jenny is coauthor of *Welcoming the Stranger* and a contributing author to three other books.

I met Chantou, then a twenty-three-year-old refugee, in 2017, when she was resettled in the Baltimore area by World Relief. It was during the height of the crisis when a record number of refugees were fleeing violence and conflict in her home country. The United States was resettling a small number of these individuals. Chantou was resettled by herself to start her life anew. As an adult refugee, she had to leave behind family members and try to rebuild her life alone. In my early conversations with her, she said she missed her friends and her village, and she desired to pursue her dream of becoming an architect.

Chantou is one of the millions of refugees worldwide who were forced to flee from their homes due to violence and persecution. She lost four of her close childhood friends to bombings and violence in her home country. When we had conversations about God, she said that while she was raised Muslim, she left religion because she doesn't believe in a God who would perpetuate war.

Violence comes in many forms. Some face violence in the shadow of stealth military drones dropping bombs on their villages. For others, the violence is more personal and comes in the form of abuse from a loved one, friend, or a family member. The effects of violence are devastating, as people face trauma, loss, and pain.

Conflict, violence, and exploitation account for much of the human suffering in the world. Whether the problem is hunger, displacement, or disease, it can often be traced back to conflict. And it's a cycle that feeds off itself, as conflict breeds poverty and poverty breeds conflict. God reminds us through this psalm, however, that those who carry out violence, those who "draw the sword and bend the bow," are wicked, and that those who pursue violence will not stand. In fact, their actions will be thwarted, and they will inflict harm on themselves in the process.

Finding Peace in the God of Hope

Some people may question the existence of God because of the world's suffering, but astute Bible readers know that following Jesus doesn't mean that suffering goes away or that violence ceases. In fact, Jesus teaches his disciples to "love [our] enemies and pray for those who persecute [us, and in this way, we prove that we are the] children of [our] Father in heaven" (Matt. 5:44–45). Our God "causes his sun to rise on the evil and the good, and sends rain on the righteous and the unrighteous" (v. 45). God also gives us grace in our difficult circumstances, so that we know we are not alone. Therefore, hope increases because he promises to defend those who experience violence (Deut. 32:35; Rom. 12:17–21). "Vengeance is mine," says the Lord (Rom. 12:19).

God sees and knows all. His omniscience gives us peace that he is ultimately in control of all things, while his omnipresence provides comfort amid our suffering, for the suffering servant is always near to the brokenhearted and those who are crushed in spirit (Ps. 34:18). Because God grants us peace, we can become peacemakers and trust him, even in the face of violence. The whole Bible demonstrates God's heart for peace and his desire for humans to turn away from violence to foster and cultivate peace whenever and wherever possible. This biblical understanding allows us to build bridges, create common ground, and cultivate empathy and unity where divisions tend to exist.

Pursuing Peace in the Face of Violence

In 2012, I visited the Democratic Republic of Congo (DRC), a beautiful, resource-rich country called "the heart of Africa" where a brutal and continuous conflict has spanned over two decades and has taken millions of lives. In this conflict, considered one of the deadliest since World War II, women and children are often most affected, as they are forcibly recruited into armed groups and experience many forms of gross physical violence. Rape is regularly used as a weapon of war, and that can have a direct impact in the lives of children. In the Democratic Republic of Congo, as in many other parts of the world, armed conflict has become more profitable than peace.

But throughout the world, God has also placed peacemakers like my colleague Marcel, who serves his community and shepherds leaders through our local World Relief office in the DRC. Together, they are actively fighting for justice: placing their faith and belief in a God who is just and trusting him to break the bow of the wicked.

Whenever I ask Marcel about his motivation, he talks about the extensive narrative of peace in the Bible and how he believes that his actions are ultimately an extension of what Christ has done for him. He fundamentally believes that the local church, through the power of the Holy Spirit, can be the hands and feet of Jesus, bringing healing, reconciliation, and peace to a people who know violence and suffering too well.

A Call to Peaceful Action

We often think of peace as a natural state of being, but the reality is that we must pursue it and create it. Nelson Mandela once said, "Peace is not just the absence of conflict; peace is the creation of an environment where all can flourish, regardless of race, color, creed, religion, gender, class, caste, or any other social markers of difference."[1] This is why 1 Peter 3:11 instructs us to "turn from evil and do good; [we] must seek peace and pursue it." Like peacemakers in the DRC, we cannot simply wait for peace; we must wage peace.

> We cannot simply wait for peace; we must wage peace.

Believing that God is the ultimate arbiter of justice gives us the freedom to pursue peace. Knowing that God is with us and that he sees every injustice allows us to lament and proclaim his kingdom come while actively working to change the circumstances around us. The power of the Holy Spirit and the truth of the Bible embolden believers to set our faces like flint to stand against violence, knowing that the Lord is able and willing to help. Therefore, we "will not be put to shame" (Isa. 50:7). This assurance also gives us the freedom to accept the outcome even if we don't see the fruit of our efforts.

Amid so much suffering and violence in the world, God offers us hope that he is just; he will avenge, and he has the final word. At a time when over 1.6 million people worldwide lose their lives to violence every year,[2] the church must lead in breaking cycles of violence by "bending the bow" of peace, by sharing the hope found in God's love, and by pursuing justice for all people. Peace deserves more than a chance; peace is not just a utopian idea. It is a divine calling from our Creator, so we must fight for it.

Dear God, we acknowledge you as our loving Father and worship you for being the God of mercy and the God of justice. We know that you are grieved at the violence in our world. Give us strength to become peacemakers who are willing to love our neighbors and our enemies. Help us become a people who shines a light in the darkest places. May your healing and comfort come quickly to those who are sick, hurting, and vulnerable. We love you. Amen.

Gyeong Ju Son (A Living Historical Figure)

A North Korean Refugee Story

We are all making history every day of our lives. For Women of Color, our stories are often connected to those of our families and are shaped within the context of our larger communities. Sometimes we share them in the privacy of our homes, and at other times we carry them in silence, and as a result, they are forgotten. I lift up this story so that the Korean refugees, young and old, are never forgotten.

Gyeong Ju Son is a North Korean refugee who was born in Pyong-yang, the capital city of North Korea. She is the only child of a wealthy family, and her father was an assistant to Kim Jong-Un, the dictator of North Korea. Having a family member closely associated with the dictator meant certain access and privileges, but it also meant greater scrutiny over her family's every move. When she was six years old, her family was targeted and persecuted by the North Korean government. They fled to China in 1998.

After settling in China, they started attending church. Shortly thereafter, her mother—who was pregnant with her second child—passed away from leukemia, and Gyeong Ju was left as an only child. Amid this tragedy, her father started a Bible study with missionaries from China and the United States. Gyeong Ju's father desired to become a missionary. However, in 2001, he was arrested and deported back to North Korea and then sentenced to prison, leaving Gyeong Ju behind. After his release from prison, Gyeong Ju's father decided against going to South Korea, where he could have enjoyed religious freedom and safety; instead, he decided to share the gospel with the people of his homeland, North Korea. In 2006, his work was discovered by the North Korean government and he was imprisoned, never to be heard from again.

Gyeong Ju was adopted by the family of a Chinese pastor, and they immigrated to the United States in 2007. Later, she went to South Korea to study. In 2010, she was asked to speak at the Lausanne Cape Town Congress.[3] After sharing her testimony, she was offered a full scholarship to Biola University, where she received her bachelor's degree and met her husband.

Gyeong Ju has a desire to go back to South Korea to start a business to help North Korean refugees with their education and other skills. She believes that even though Korea remains divided today, there is one Korea. Gyeong Ju has dedicated her life to helping the people of North Korea, and in the face of violence, she is a peacemaker who is using her faith to build bridges between two places and two peoples. There are tens of thousands of vulnerable North Korean refugees in China, and leaders like Gyeong Ju give us hope that there will eventually be peace on the Korean peninsula.

TWELVE

Just One Suitcase

Better the little that the righteous have
than the wealth of many wicked;
for the power of the wicked will be broken,
but the LORD upholds the righteous.

Psalm 37:16–17

Lisa Rodriguez-Watson is the national director of Missio
Alliance. She also serves as the associate pastor of discipleship
and equipping at Christ City Church. A proud Cuban American,
Lisa is an activist for immigration reform. She is a writer and
conference speaker. Lisa lives in Washington, DC, with her
husband and three kids.

I t must have been so difficult to leave her life, her friends, her family and have only one suitcase to take with her," I remarked to my *abuela* as we talked about her sister, Raquel, who had recently defected from Cuba to the United States while on a government trip.

With tenderness and conviction, she responded, "Lisa, *asi fue como salimos todos, con una sola maleta en nuestras manos*" [Lisa, that's how we all left, with just one suitcase in our hands]. I was stunned to think about the enormous sacrifice it was for my grandparents to flee with their three young boys, one a mere infant, to begin a new life in the United States.

After months of requests to the government and consistent denials for visas for the entire family, my grandfather was finally granted five visas on Christmas Eve 1961. "Here are your family's visas. Pack your things; you leave tomorrow" were the astounding words of the Cuban official.

Imagine uprooting your entire life and leaving your home in one day. Imagine saying goodbye to your parents, sisters, brothers, friends, and neighbors all in one afternoon, not knowing, because of a war and economic factors, when or if you will ever see them again. Imagine selecting clothes for yourself, your husband, and your kids that will be sufficient for the life that awaits you on a new shore, and yet modest enough to fit in your suitcases. Imagine your conversations with God throughout that day as you say goodbye. Imagine your salty, bittersweet tears and deepest heart groans of joy and lament making their way heavenward to the God who sees and knows you.

Abuelita's Perspective

I wonder if it was the "one suitcase" reality that gave my family the perspective they shared with me in my growing-up years? Occasionally, my *abuela* would fold up a twenty-dollar bill and press it into my hand as I was leaving her house after a visit. Curious about why she was giving me money and not keeping it for herself, I would ask her about it. She would respond with a simple and frank, "*Para que lo necesito yo? Dios me ha dado todo de lo que necesito*" [What do I need it for? God has given me what I need]. Despite never amassing any wealth, she seemed free of the clutches of greed and material affluence. Through her generosity, she quietly lived in prophetic opposition to the machinations of excess that are so prevalent here in the United States.

a vida es la lucha

Perhaps she understood the first verse of the passage from Psalm 37 quoted above: "Better the little that the righteous have than the wealth of many wicked." In a world that screams, "Get as much as you can at any cost," rings the clarion call of truth that reorients us to real abundance and the justice of God. The pursuit of material gain is rarely regarded positively in Scripture. Instead, Scripture calls us to an abundance of virtues like generosity, humility, faith, and righteousness. In the eyes of the world, these merits matter less. In God's economy, however, they are the assets most prized. They are the ingredients that make for a beautiful life. Of all the things to treasure, these gems are what we pack into our "one suitcase" of life.

Jesus echoes and clarifies this upside-down economy of God in the Beatitudes. "Blessed are you who are poor, for yours is the kingdom of God" (Luke 6:20). Those who have little, the broke and broken down, are the ones who gain an inheritance beyond worth, measure, and imagination. Though their earthly possessions may fit into just one suitcase, their heavenly Father bestows on them blessing and the abundance of the kingdom. By contrast, consider how the rich young ruler walked away sad from Jesus, because he could not comprehend surrendering his material possessions to receive the spiritual rewards that a life with Jesus offers.

The exhortation is also an invitation. The psalmist and Jesus invite us into a way of living that sees our sufficiency in Christ. They beckon us into a life that is full, not with the stuff of earth but with the stuff of the kingdom, where love, joy, peace, patience, kindness, goodness, faithfulness, gentleness, and self-control are the hallmarks (Gal. 5:22–23). The psalmist and Jesus call us to intertwine our lives with the lives of those experiencing poverty—those marginalized and ground down by the world's powerful and prosperous—for it is in proximity to and in relationship with the poor that we might learn something rich about our Lord.

I am my *abuela*'s granddaughter, and I am a daughter of the values in this country that my family now calls home. The tide of American dreaming has made its way into my life, and I find myself interrogating my situation. I have more than I can fit into hundreds of suitcases. I own a home. Without intention, I can isolate myself from those in my city who are struggling economically and are being oppressed by economic and justice systems. I need to continually return to the words of Jesus, to the words of Scripture, to my *abuela*'s words, lest I drift into the toxic stream that seduces me into thinking that satisfaction is determined by comforts and security is found by the way of wealth.

Mi Familia's Legacy

I am proud to belong to the Rodriguez family, one whose heart beats for the righteousness and justice of God's kingdom. I am proud to be the daughter of an immigrant whose prayers, hard work, and persistence have made an indelible mark on me. That deep pride of being both a Jesus follower and a descendant of an immigrant family fuels a profound lament for the ways our country disregards and oppresses its immigrants. What's more lamentable still is the white evangelical church's complicity and acquiescence in this oppression. The Scriptures are clear that God has a unique concern for the widow, the orphan, the poor, and the immigrant. Any attempt to disparage or neglect the image of God in immigrants, as in all humanity, is, as the psalmist writes, "wickedness."

The psalmist is clear in these verses that God upholds the righteous and that the power of the wicked will be broken. In my lament, I am met with the comfort and truth of God's faithfulness as a sustainer of his people. Likewise, my lament is eased when I am reminded of God's power to destroy the wicked. It is not mine to determine the timing or manner of God enacting this justice, but I hold hope and faith together in our God, who will accomplish justice in the earth.

Because of the beautiful faith and legacy of *mi familia*, I have come to understand and aim for the beauty of a life lived from "one suitcase." May we be found faithful pursuing the upside-down kingdom, where less is more and righteousness is of great gain over the wealth of the wicked.

Dear Jesus, we lament the brokenness of this world that forces families to flee their homes and their lands. We lament the ways immigrants are often treated in our communities. We pray for your justice. Give us eyes to see you among the poor and to see our own depravity when we pursue worldly gain at any cost. Grant that we would value simplicity with righteousness over abundance with wickedness. We pray this for the sake of your kingdom and in your name. Amen.

Ada María Isasi-Díaz (1943–2012)

Always in the Struggle

Ada María Isasi-Díaz was born in Havana, Cuba, in 1943. She grew up in a large family with her two parents and seven siblings. Her groundbreaking *Mujerista* theology has its roots in her earliest years, during which she learned about staying in the struggle (*siguiendo en la lucha*) for what one believes.

Years of civil war and revolution forced her family to make the unfortunate and heartbreaking decision to leave their homeland. When she was seventeen, she and her family arrived in the United States as political refugees and made their home in Louisiana. She entered the Order of St. Ursula, and by her midtwenties made the decision to move to Lima, Peru, for three years as a missionary with the Ursulines.[1]

In reflecting on her time in Peru, Isasi-Díaz wrote, "This experience marked me for life. . . . It was there that the poor taught me the gospel message of justice. It was there that I learned to respect and admire the religious understandings and practices of the poor and the oppressed and the importance of their everyday struggles, of *lo cotidiano*. It was there that I realized the centrality of solidarity with the poor and the oppressed in the struggle for justice."[2]

As the mother of *Mujerista* theology, which centers the experiences of Latinas, especially the poor, in embodying Christian faith in the everyday *luchas* ("struggles") of life, Isasi-Díaz empowered countless women theologians. She acknowledged that Latinas must come to understand the reality of structural sin and find ways to combat it, because the effect of structural sin hides God's ongoing revelation from us and from society at large.[3]

It was her love of *Jesucristo* that fueled her passion for shaping a feminist liberation theology for Latinas in the United States. She called for the constant evaluation of the theological enterprise by intentionally asking whom it benefits. She believed in a loving God who can break the power of the wicked and whose Spirit is able to transform systemic oppression into systemic justice when humanity works together to lift the poor and vulnerable.

She lost the fight against an aggressive form of cancer in May 2012. In the wake of her loss now lives a legacy of empowerment of Latinas and women, care for the poor, and the wholehearted truth that *la vida es la lucha* ("to struggle is to live").[4]

STROPHE 4

PSALM 37:18–22

THIRTEEN

Alpha and Omega

A Poem by Mazaré, African American Spoken-Word Poet

Armied ankles allied to antagonize
abide, awarded amnesty.

African agents.
American authorities.
Apart. Abroad.

Both blasting brown bodies.

Bouncy bullets. Baton blows.
Badges bilk bagfuls of bounty.

Children commanded to cede
cameras, clothes, cars.

Duty to defend defenseless
defied.

Enraged emerge.
#EndSARS, #EndRacism,
Exploiting, Extorting, Eating.

Fangs focus on faithful,
fouling flags flowing

Greenwhitegreen.
Glowingredwhiteblue.

Holy hands hang heavy.
Harbor holes
and heat.

Irons.
Jaded by jackals jilting justice.
Knotted knowing knock-off kings kneel on knecks.

Lekki languishing.
Larcenia Floyd's lad lying lifeless.

Lily, listen.
Law lizards lack longevity.

Muscle's mere meat.
Money melts.

Naija, nobility now neglecting natives
Omega *ordained* to be overthrown.

Public and private profiteers,
pulverized,

Prejudiced pythons—
Painted protectors
Quit by quills.
Ruthless ravagers razed,
roots
Scissored.

Trust, though *they* triumph today,
Undergrounders
Vault victorious.
Wailers will win,
whistling with
Xylophones
Your youth to
Zenith.

From the poet: "Alpha and Omega" was inspired by the movements to #EndRacism in America, to #EndSARS in Nigeria, and to end police brutality in both. The Special Anti-Robbery Squad (SARS) is a branch of the Nigerian police that was founded in 1992 to combat armed robbery and fraud, and became a perpetrator of those exact crimes and more against the Nigerian people. In recent years, the violent repression and murder of peaceful protestors has spurred a worldwide movement to bring an end to the abuse of power and the exploitation of the people of Nigeria carried out by their government.

From the editor: Psalm 37 is an alphabetical acrostic poem following the twenty-two letters of the Hebrew alphabet. One purpose of this technique is for memorization, or for the readers or any hearer to recall the information presented to the community. Mazaré brilliantly follows this formula by outlining her poem using the twenty-six letters of the English alphabet.

Mazaré is an African American spoken-word poet who describes herself as raw honey, "a teaspoon of brutal truth fresh from the comb—bold and thick with sweet." She is the community life coordinator at Grace Downtown in Washington, DC.

FOURTEEN

Walking Blameless in the Dark

The blameless spend their days under the LORD's care,
and their inheritance will endure forever.
In times of disaster they will not wither;
in days of famine they will enjoy plenty.

Psalm 37:18–19

Natasha Sistrunk Robinson is the president of T3 Leadership Solutions, Inc., and the visionary founder of the 501(c)(3) non-profit Leadership LINKS, Inc. This African American woman from South Carolina is an author, host of *A Sojourner's Truth* podcast, speaker, consultant, and coach who engages, equips, and empowers people to live and lead on purpose.

Blameless is the Black woman in America, not perfect in her own right, not without flaws, not divine, but blameless. She is African American only because her ancestors were taken from a continent that is no longer her own and enslaved. She bore the darkness and trauma of the slave ship. She did not embrace the darkness of death while at sea. She survived and arrived in this new land, where she was shamed and stripped of her identity—where her Black body, breasts, and private parts were exposed—and was put on an auction block for public display

121

and consumption. How much is her Black body worth? The psalmist writes that Yahweh knows the days of the blameless and promises them an inheritance. *What does the Bible mean by blameless?*

The Hebrew word for blameless in this passage is *tamim*. It refers to a person who is righteous, walks upright, or is innocent in conduct. According to the Bible, a blameless person is *content* that God knows the real, and she is *confident* that God will respond accordingly to the wicked. It's a character statement referencing her faithful response to the truth that she knows, in spite of the reality that she experiences.

The Darkness of Slavery

El Roi is the name Hagar, an enslaved Egyptian woman, cried out from the wilderness. She was the property of the chosen one, Abram, and his wife, Sarai (Gen. 16). God is no respecter of persons (Acts 10:34 KJV), and Abram and his people were no better than her. God chooses whom he chooses. That's God's business. Hagar was abused, raped, and "knocked up"—that's the phrase Black folks use to describe having a child "out of order" from an unholy union.

It was Sarai who was barren and could not bear children. It was the matriarch, Sarai, who orchestrated the plan to get her husband into bed with another woman. Hagar was not the jezebel, and when the inevitable happened, Hagar despised Sarai for it (Gen. 16:4). It is one thing to have your body taken, but now, Sarai had taken her womb. Sarai is queen, and Abram is being played like a chess piece. He doesn't care about Hagar; she was just an easy lay. So, he says to his wife, "Your slave is in your hands. . . . Do with her whatever you think is best" (v. 6). After all, he is a man of means in a patriarchal society. He will be okay with or without sons, but not Sarai. Her quality of life and security depend on her husband's ability to stay alive and her ability to bear sons. Hagar knows that this child will not be her own, and Sarai will take him too.

After suffering the abuse and mistreatment of Sarai, this blameless woman flees to the desert. There the angel of God meets her, calls her by name, acknowledges her social location, and asks her a profound question: "Hagar, slave of Sarai, where have you come from, and where are you going?" (v. 8).

The question is not rhetorical. It conjures the voice of Diana Ross, singing, "Do you know where you're going to? Do you like the things that life is showing you?"[1] The answer is a resounding "No!"

"I'm running away from my mistress, Sarai" (v. 8). The angel sends her back to the house, under the authority of the mistress and a system that is not working for her. Yet, he sends her with a promise and an inheritance. She will be blessed. She will have a son and many descendants. Her first son's name, Ishmael, gives an account of what is transpiring: *God hears.* "The Lord has heard of your misery" (v. 11). Then this woman responds by doing something historic. She is the first human in the Bible who names God, "*El Roi.*" She says, "You are the God who sees me. . . . I have now seen the One who sees me" (Gen. 16:13). Oh, what a blessing it is to know and see the God who sees me!

God's Response to the Blameless

Blamelessness is always about God. First, it is a very practical claim that God is not simply concerned with spiritual things. God hears the cries of the enslaved woman. God cares about her life and her body, both of which are holy and set apart for God's good purposes. God cares about how we name her, the stories we tell about her, and about the systemic injustices of white supremacy and misogyny. Therefore, we must question the historical account of the white, patriarchal gaze that has been empowered to name the enslaved African woman mammy, jezebel, sapphire, and matriarch. We must reject every lie that tells us to hate and blame her, and for her to hate herself. We must stand in solidarity with Hagar to see herself as God sees her.

The words of Toni Morrison beckon us to love her and, as Black women in America, to love ourselves. Morrison writes, "In this here place, we flesh; flesh that weeps, laughs; flesh that dances on bare feet in grass. Love it, love it hard. Yonder they do not love your flesh. They despise it."[2] She compels us to love the dark eyes; the dark skin on our backs; our dark hands; our dark faces. You are to love; your dark mouth; your dark body; your dark feet; your dark shoulders; your dark, strong arms; your dark neck.[3] Love it. Love all of it! She reminds us that we must love the inside parts too: the dark liver, the beating heart, the lungs, the life-holding womb, and the life-giving private parts.[4] Love it, for this is our inheritance and our prize.[5]

God is love and our eternal inheritance. Love makes us blameless and complete. There is no shame in loving oneself. The greatest commandment says that we are to love our neighbors *as* we love ourselves.[6] This is the way that the blameless honor God. The psalmist predicts that the blameless will not be ashamed in the time of evil. In the worst darkness, exerting Black love, Black dignity, and justice for Black lives has been ours. Seeking reconciliation between every human relationship that was broken in the Bible can be ours. Blameless is knowing that we have first been reconciled to God and understanding that our inheritance with Christ has given us the ministry of reconciliation (2 Cor. 5:18). Dr. Chanequa Walker-Barnes defines racial reconciliation as

> part of God's ongoing and eschatological mission to restore wholeness and peace to a world broken by systemic injustice. Racial

reconciliation focuses its effort upon dismantling White supremacy, the systemic evil that denies and distorts the image of God
inherent in all humans based upon the heretical belief that White
aesthetics, values, and cultural norms bear the fullest representation of the *imago Dei*.[7]

White supremacy is an idol that results in wicked behavior and
violent assaults against God and the *imago Dei*. Black women are
blameless, standing complete in God because we too bear the image
of God. We serve *El Roi*. In the vein of the well-known spiritual, "Nobody knows the trouble the Black woman has seen. Nobody knows
but Jesus."

The psalmist David wrote that God keeps a record of our sorrows, collects all our tears in a bottle, and records each one in his
book (Ps. 56:8). In the darkness of grief and injustice, Black women
have carried the memories of our slain, sustained movements, raised
children, and prioritized our faith. David wrote that when facing
evildoers, the blameless spend their days in the Lord's care. Black
mothers have kept us in the church. With love and respect for our
Black men, we can acknowledge that Black women have often carried our communities and the struggles for justice in our bodies and
on our backs, but there will come a day when the wicked will cease
from causing trouble and the weary will be at rest (Job 3:17). Though
weary, blameless Black women persistently work toward this peace.

God's Promised Inheritance

God grants peace in the middle of the storm. "Weeping may endure
for a night, but joy comes in the morning" (Ps. 30:5 NKJV). The storm
may not be in the wee hours, and morning may not be a sleep and
a wake-up. Morning may not even be tomorrow. In the same way

that we affirm, "Jesus is coming soon" (Rev. 22:20, paraphrase), we understand that "soon" is not an exact time but rather a designated one. Peter reminds us not to forget "dear friends: With the Lord a day is like a thousand years, and a thousand years are like a day" (2 Pet. 3:8). Therefore, the inheritance referenced in Psalm 37:18–19 reminds us of the predictions that are sure to come in due time. Those who walk blameless *will* have an inheritance that lasts forever. They *will not* be ashamed in the time of evil. And in the darkness, when we look over the many years of injustice that blameless Black women have endured, the promise is they *will* be satisfied. The blameless will be complete, lacking no good thing (Ps 34:10). So, as we cry and lament, we women must remember to walk in our inheritance. Remember God's call to love, God's ministry of reconciliation, and God's redemption. Morning is coming, sistas. Jesus is on the way.

El Roi, you bring light where there is darkness. You exchange beauty for ashes. You give us a hopeful future. You are the God of all comfort. Draw near to me now. Gather my prayers and tears. Make me blameless. In Jesus's name. Amen.

Sojourner Truth (1797–1883)

A Blameless Black Woman

Ain't I a woman? When I heard the name Sojourner Truth as a child, this question stuck to and smeared it like white glue on black construction paper. Supposedly, she rhetorically asked this question about her identity during a famous speech in 1851. I knew that Sojourner Truth was an orator, but it wasn't until adulthood that I learned she never spoke the words "Ar'n't I a Woman?" Those words were crafted by the white feminist writer Frances Dana Gage.

The real Sojourner Truth is a woman, of course, and her life tells a deeper story. In 1797, she was born in Ulster County, New York, as Isabella, daughter of farmers, Elizabeth (Mau Mau Bett) and James (Bomefree). Elizabeth was a devout woman who gathered her children, reassuring them, "'There is a God, who hears and sees you. . . . When you are beaten, or cruelly treated, or fall into any trouble, you must ask help of him, and he will always hear and help you.' . . . She endeavor[ed] to show them their Heavenly Father, as the only being who could protect them in their perilous condition."[8] The simple message of the blameless is knowing that there is a God who hears and sees, and God is the only one who can protect you and make you complete in him.

Although slavery was abolished in the state of New York in 1799, the Emancipation Act was gradual. In 1810, around age nine, Isabella was purchased by John Dumont. She later married Thomas, who was an enslaved man, and together they had five children. Isabella negotiated the terms of her early emancipation but left in 1826 when her owner failed to free her as promised. In that same year, her master illegally sold her five-year-old-son, Peter, down south to Alabama. She took his case to court and won!

Although separated from her family for much of her adult life, she continued to spend her days under the Lord's care. She was illiterate, never learning to read or write. Yet empowered by the Holy Spirit, she became a dynamic preacher and an advocate for women's rights, the abolition of slavery, and voting rights for both communities. She renamed herself Sojourner Truth on June 1, 1843, understanding that "a sojourner is someone not at home, and truth is what preachers impart."[9] She first published her narrative in 1850. Like Harriet Tubman, she provided support to the Union Army during the Civil War. When meeting with President Lincoln, she advocated for newly freed Blacks to receive land from the government.

Although her story has often been fashioned by others outside her ethnic group, Sojourner Truth's life reveals the importance and power of submitting to the Holy Spirit as we assert our full and embodied identities in public. In times of darkness, this Black, poor, formerly enslaved woman without a formal education did not wither. Instead, in the words of Tupac, she became as a rose that grew up from concrete.[10] When the world did not esteem her, she imaged her Savior, who *grew up like a tender shoot, like a root out of dry ground, who had no beauty or majesty that was attractive by the world's standards, who was despised and rejected by humankind, and who suffered and was familiar with pain* (Isa. 53:2–3, paraphrase). As a portrait and historical figure, she still stands publicly exerting her dignity, her beauty, and her Blackness in her gendered body. She stands blameless to remind us of the flowing water and daily manna that God's care provides amid famine. That is holy representation of a blameless Black woman, and that is plenty.

FIFTEEN

The Wicked Will Perish

But the wicked will perish:
    Though the LORD's enemies are like the flowers of
        the field,
    they will be consumed, they will go up in smoke.

Psalm 37:20

Michelle Ami Reyes is an Indian American author, speaker, and writer. She is the vice president of the Asian American Christian Collaborative and the co-executive director of Pax. She is also the Scholar-in-Residence at Hope Community Church in East Austin, where her husband, Aaron, serves as lead pastor. She is the author of *Becoming All Things: How Small Changes Lead to Lasting Connections Across Cultures.*

There is an old Indian tale called "The Cruel Crane Outwitted." The story goes that a hungry young crane deceives an entire pond of fish, promising them passage in his mouth from their small habitat to a much greater lake, but it is nothing more than a ruse to eat them. Each time the crane scoops up a fish, he takes it to a tree, where he murders it and eats its flesh. Over the years, no one ever wises up to the crane, and his pile of fish bones grows ever larger until one day all the fish are dead and eaten. The crane, being greedy, tries to then deceive a crab from the same pond, but the crab outwits him. Right as the crane is about to throw the crab on the heap of fish bones and eat it, the crab clamps down on the bird's neck with its pincers and kills the bird instead. A villager nearby witnesses the event and concludes the tale by saying, "The villain, though exceedingly clever, shall not prosper by his villainy. He may win indeed, sharp-witted in deceit, but only as the crane here from the crab."[1]

I grew up reading tales like "The Cruel Crane Outwitted," and even at a young age, I found that folklore from India helped illuminate so many truths in Scripture that it just made sense to read them side by side. In fact, I can't think of a more fitting representation of the wicked perishing as illustrated in Psalm 37:20 than in this tale. Certainly, like many tales within folklore, God's Word promises that all will end justly, with the righteous rewarded and the wicked punished. Justice, however, is not immediately administered. The fish in the tale remain dead. In Psalm 37, similarly, the righteous cry out to God, questioning whether to believe in good and whether good will eventually win in the world. Psalm 37:20 is God's assured reply: *the wicked will perish.*

The End Is Near

There is nothing more gut-wrenching than the wicked prospering on this earth. In our world, corruption is rampant, evils such as racism and systemic injustice thrive, and the gap between dominant and subdominant cultures continues to widen. The poor, the marginalized, and the hurting are helplessly trapped by schemes and false promises, while those who perpetuate the cycle of violence and oppression satiate themselves with privilege, status, and wealth.

Throughout Psalm 37, we see the righteous experience emotions of frustration and anger that are deeply troubling. They continuously wonder how much more injustice they must endure. You can feel the weight of their despair. The wicked are more successful than they are. In fact, the wicked are thriving at the expense of the righteous. The response of God's people is to question God's sovereignty. *Is he even in control?*

The state of the righteous in the ancient Near East resembles the plight of subdominant cultures in the US today. Many Asian Americans know hardship and oppression firsthand. Like that of the fish in "The Cruel Crane Outwitted," their vulnerable status causes them to fall prey to the deceit and corruption of the cranes of society. Those who have power and know how to manipulate it claim to offer prosperity and a better way of life, but in reality, their words are nothing but lies that inevitably harm our bodies and livelihoods. The promises of safety for assimilating and becoming white proximate did not save Vincent Chin,[2] beaten to death by two white men at his own bachelor party, or prevent the 1871 Chinese Massacre,[3] the largest mass lynching in American history in which eighteen Chinese men were hanged by an angry white mob. In 2017, a white male shooter shouted, "Get out of my country,"[4] as he fatally shot Srinivas Kuchibhotla and wounded Alok Madasani, two Indian nationals, while also injuring the gentleman who tried to apprehend him at a restaurant in northeastern Kansas.

The bombing of the World Trade Center catalyzed an increase in anti-Indian racism as many were misidentified as Middle Easterners. I remember, as a fifteen-year-old girl, being called a "terrorist" in the week following the attack. Other Indian families had their cars keyed. From the 1882 Chinese Exclusion Act to the reality now of living in a post-9/11 society and the age of COVID-19, Asians have gone "from pet to threat," in the words of Dr. Soong-Chan Rah.[5] Dr. Russell Jeung also puts it succinctly: "We went from being Crazy Rich Asians—the model minority—to Crazy Infected Asians:

disease carriers, national security threats, and perpetual foreigners."[6] Despite Asian American efforts to pursue the American dream like their white colleagues and neighbors and reach the idyllic lake, we still suffer from a long history of oppression and erasure within US American history. Anti-Asian racism abounds, and yet justice rarely comes for the Asian American. This is a wickedness that runs rampant, and Asian Americans across this country continue to cry out, "How long, O Lord?"

Like a folktale that is passed from one storyteller to the next, Psalm 37 contains the answer that an old, wise person gives to a younger generation. The truth of Psalm 37:20 is simple: *Yes, the wicked will perish*. Though they may enjoy prosperity for the moment, their exploitation and oppression will have their fateful end.

The psalmist compares the wicked to flowers. Though they may be beautiful now, like grass in a fire, they will eventually go up in smoke and be destroyed.

I live in Austin, Texas, and every March our family looks forward to Texas wildflowers ushering in the spring with their splashes of bright, beautiful colors. Gorgeous bluebonnets and Indian paintbrush line the roads and spread lazily across people's yards. It's a glorious sight to behold, but you have to enjoy it fast, because in April, the Texas heat rises and the wildflowers meet a swift, scorched end. These flowers enjoy only temporary flourishing. This is why Psalm 37:16 also says, "Better the little that the righteous have than the wealth of many wicked." The earthly comfort of the wicked will not equate to eternal comfort. We can rest assured that there is a reckoning coming of fire, judgment, and destruction. Make no mistake, the fury of hell is coming for the wicked.

During the onset of the COVID-19 global pandemic, Dr. Russell Jeung organized the Stop AAPI Hate reporting center. He wanted to prove to policymakers and the broader American public that

Asian Americans indeed face racism. The flood of incidents in the span of one year was horrific and disheartening. From March to October 2020, they received over twenty-six hundred reports from forty-seven states and Washington, DC, ranging from civil rights violations and verbal harassment to spitting, coughing, and physical assaults.[7] Few of the perpetrators have been arrested, let alone charged. The heavy reality is that on this side of glory, the wicked—those who undermine the image of God in their fellow humans, those who commit racist acts and perpetuate racist rhetoric and systems—often prosper. Though they engage in the dastardliest schemes, they often thrive from an earthly perspective. There are days when it feels like there will never be an end to discrimination and hostility; that racists will not be punished for their crimes; that anti-racist policies will never go into effect; and that the hearts and minds of people against Asians will never soften. Justice has not yet come for Asian Americans; instead, we continue to suffer under the weight of mental health struggles, racial trauma, and disprivilege like so many people of color in the United States.

Relief, however, is coming! Psalm 37:20 promises us that the wicked will perish. Justice is coming, but it may not be in our lifetime. We must hope and wait. We may actually suffer and even die unjustly. Nonetheless, we must place our hope in God's coming justice.

Don't Despair

The theme of flowers in Psalm 37:20 echoes Jesus's teaching in the Sermon on the Mount. In Matthew 6:25–34, Jesus describes flowers as "here today and tomorrow thrown into the fire" (v. 30). But more importantly, he uses the imagery of flowers to exhort his followers not to worry. God always has and always will take care of them. When we read the Psalms and Matthew 6 side by side, we can better understand Psalm 37's implication that the wicked do not *deserve* our strong emotions, for in reality, they are as short-lived as plants that quickly wither away (v. 2; Ps. 103:15–16). We may not be able to control or change the present, but we can control our own emotions. We can choose hope and trust in God instead of anger, bitterness, and despair.

It's an odd thing to say, but there's hope and comfort in knowing that the wicked will perish someday. As Proverbs 11:10 says, "When the righteous prosper, the city rejoices; when the wicked perish, there are shouts of joy." Granted, we do not rejoice in human perishing. In fact, we must never celebrate the death or destruction of a fellow image bearer. In Ezekiel 33:11, God says, "I take no pleasure in the death of the wicked." We should always desire that our fellow human beings repent, confess their sins, come to Jesus, and turn from their wicked ways. Our hope is rooted in the joy that injustice will someday be no more. We can praise God that he will break the cycles of violence and evil and that one day the actions of the wicked will never be able to harm another person ever again.

A day is coming when racist policies and laws will be no more. On that day, Black and Brown bodies will not be shot in the streets. Asian aunties won't have acid thrown in their faces. Children won't be chased down roads and taunted with the words "Go back home to your country." One day, there will be no more cruel cranes to pluck fish from their homes and murder them in high trees. One day, oppressors will be no more and all tears will be wiped from our eyes. On that day, wickedness will come to an end, and that is the hope we *must* cling to.

Oh, Lord, we cry out, "Maranatha."[8] *Come, Lord, come. May you return soon and bring an end to the wickedness of this world. But should you tarry and the days remain long, equip us with the truth*

134

of your promises so that we may endure. We know that the wicked will one day perish. You will act as a righteous judge and bring their evil to a swift end. But in the meantime, while evil and injustice continue to prevail, protect us from unholy anger, bitterness, and despair. Bring your relief, we pray. Maranatha.

Pandita Ramabai (1858–1922)

A Woman Who Stared Wickedness in the Face

A young girl stood before Pandita Ramabai, helpless and alone. The girl, now barely twelve, had been married off at age five and had recently become a child widow. According to Brahmin custom, she would not be allowed to remarry. In fact, this young girl would now be considered cursed, and she would be required to shave her head, wear drab clothes, and eat only meager food. Widows in India were and still are subject to physical and sexual abuse. Ramabai, a child widow herself, knew that this girl was doomed to a lifetime on the margins, and that realization catalyzed her life's work. Recalling that first meeting, Ramabai wrote, "As I looked on that little figure my vague thoughts about doing something for my sisters in similar conditions began to take shape [and] I began to place a plan for starting a home for Hindu widows before my countrymen and to ask for their help."[9]

Pandita Ramabai was the most controversial woman of her time. Her father taught her Sanskrit, the ancient Hindu liturgical language reserved for Brahmin men. She was the rare widow who remained in public view, defying customs as an Indian woman who decided, on her own, to convert to Christianity. Considered the first Indian woman feminist, she traveled across India sharing the Good News of Jesus and giving lectures on women's rights while also drawing international attention to the plight of abused widows and starting schools that offered shelter and education to thousands of young women. Perhaps most astounding, Ramabai charted these waters as a single woman and mother.

Pandita Ramabai was born on April 23, 1858, into a Brahmin family, and her life was characterized by struggle and loss. She was only sixteen when she lost both her parents to famine. "[My] father's last loving command to me," she wrote in a letter quoted by Kosambi, "was to live an honourable life, if I lived at all, and serve God all my life."[10] When she was twenty-three, her husband died, leaving her alone with their one-year-old daughter, Manorama. Ramabai, however, was undeterred despite living within an unjust system that did not value women.

Her Christian faith compelled her to social reform and women's education. She wrote, "I realized after reading the fourth chapter of St. John's Gospel that Christ was truly the Divine Saviour he claimed to be, and no one but He could transform and uplift the downtrodden women of India. . . . Thus my heart was drawn to the religion of Christ."[11]

Not only the Word of God but also the examples of subdominant cultures in the US fueled Ramabai's activism. She deeply identified with Native Americans and African Americans. At one point, Ramabai came to the US to raise prayer and financial support for her fledgling mission. In a letter to her daughter, Ramabai describes meeting the escaped slave and abolitionist Harriet Tubman and urges Manorama to be "as helpful to her own dear country women as Harriet was and is to her own people."[12]

Using proceeds from her book and lectures, she raised funds to open the Sharada Sadan (Home of Learning) in 1889 in Bombay, offering widowed girls a refuge where they could study and learn skills like gardening, carpentry, and sewing. Over time, her shelter, which started as a strictly secular mission, became unabashedly religious. Ramabai built a church and established the Mukti (Salvation) Mission.[13] At one point, it served more than seven hundred girls and women. Many became teachers and nurses, while others stayed, running a dairy farm and their own printing press. The home is still active today.

The powerful story of Pandita Ramabai demonstrates how one woman saw needs around her and in the face of great wickedness addressed them, and as a result of those faithful actions influenced and impacted lives in India for 130 years.

SIXTEEN

Generous Like Our God

The wicked borrows but does not pay back,
> but the righteous is generous and gives;
for those blessed by the LORD shall inherit the land,
> but those cursed by him shall be cut off.

Psalm 37:21–22 ESV

Vivian Mabuni is a Chinese American speaker, author, Bible teacher, and host of the *Someday is Here* podcast for AAPI (Asian American Pacific Islander) women. Author of *Warrior in Pink: A Story of Cancer, Community, and the God Who Comforts* and *Open Hands, Willing Heart: Discover the Joy of Saying Yes to God*, Viv and her husband, Darrin, have served more than thirty years in vocational Christian ministry. They are proud parents of three young adult kids.

Throughout our study of this psalm, we see David contrast the wicked and the righteous. The clear difference in actions and attitudes should go without saying, but seeing the words inked on parchment sharply clarifies what God hates and what he honors. The virtue and blessing of the righteous are sandwiched between wickedness and curses in these two verses. Verse 21 begins, "The wicked borrows but does not pay back." Borrowing is not the issue; it is the failure to repay that results in a judgment of wickedness. It is understood that if someone borrows something, then the use of the item is temporary. Therefore, the decision to take and not pay back is rooted in selfishness, greed, and using what belongs to another to get ahead. The opposite of what is wicked is described in the second half of the verse. This posture of openhanded living is a picture of God-honoring generosity. This quality is also embedded in my Asian collective culture.

The Burrito Situation

Many years ago, my husband led a Bible study that met over lunch. These college students, all young men with extremely high metabolisms, came from a range of ethnic backgrounds. One student, Davy, regularly brought a burrito purchased from the student center food court. Davy could easily finish off the burrito by himself, but he would pull out a plastic knife, cut up his burrito, and share his lunch.

A few things to note. Davy is an Asian American, and the rest of the group was made up of young men from different ethnic heritages. For any of you unfamiliar with how a Chinese banquet works, food is shared family style. No one orders their own individual meal. If you are younger and happen to sit next to an auntie (everyone is auntie and uncle even when not blood related), she will gladly fill your plate with the biggest chunks of meat. Everyone leaves stuffed. But you will notice that at the end of the meal a single shrimp or piece of duck is always left on the platter. In an Asian American high school youth group, there's always one slice of pizza left in the box. This is because everyone considers the possibility that someone else may want the last bite.

When a group operates with the same understanding that everyone shares, the outcome is everyone gets fed. Asian Americans, like most communities of color, function with "collective" running through our cultural DNA. But we end up hungry when there is no reciprocity given from others who operate from an individualistic value system. This is why the other young men in the study didn't have a problem eating part of Davy's burrito but never thought to offer him any of their lunches. An individualistic cultural value would say, "My burrito was bought with my money—no one asked me for a bite, so I'm just eating my lunch."

Generosity

We read in the second half of verse 21: "the righteous is generous and gives." Generosity is born out of an understanding that God is the one who ultimately gives us our daily bread. In the Sermon on the Mount, Jesus teaches us not to worry about what we eat, drink, or wear because our heavenly Father knows we need these things (Matt. 6:32). Jesus effortlessly feeds the five thousand (Mark 6:30–44) by multiplying a young boy's lunch consisting of bread and fish; in the end, everyone eats until replete, and the disciples pick up twelve baskets of leftovers. In the Scriptures, we also see Jesus modeling abundant hospitality and generosity whether at a wedding turning water into wine (John 2:6–11) or making breakfast on the beach (John 21:9). Our God is a God of abundance.

As we engage in generosity, we learn quickly that we can never outgive God. Any of us who have experienced God's abundance can recall how resources and even time surprisingly multiplied when we thought our barrels empty. We bear witness to this abundance in 1 Kings 17:8–16, when reading about the prophet Elijah's food request from the widow of Zarephath during a severe famine. This woman was set to die from hunger and was preparing a final meal for herself and her son. Remarkably, Elijah obeyed God's command to ask for food from the starving widow, and the widow responded in a willingness to trust God and Elijah. She offered hospitality and food to the prophet before caring for her own family's needs. God provided through a generous miracle and saved this family and Elijah through the provision of a jar of flour and a jug of oil that never emptied. The widow of Zarephath understood that the famine impacted more than just herself and her son, so she responded by sharing with another in need.

As communities of color, we have the benefit of operating as a collective. Our culture teaches us that we are part of a greater group and that life is not about individual self-actualization or preservation. In his book *No Future Without Forgiveness*, Archbishop Desmond Tutu shares about the African value and lifestyle of *ubuntu*:

> Ubuntu is very difficult to render into a Western language. It speaks of the very essence of being human. When we want to give high praise to someone we say, "Yu, u nobuntu"; "Hey so-and-so has ubuntu." Then you are generous, you are hospitable, you are friendly and caring and compassionate. You share what you have. It is to say, "My humanity is inextricably bound up in yours." We belong in a bundle of life.[1]

We know that God is more concerned with the posture of our hearts than the actual gift that we give, and God is also concerned about people. Through *ubuntu* we see an example of how kingdom values are infused into culture to impact all creation and people's lives. Our natural bent toward the collective demonstrates kingdom generosity. The psalmist communicates the glaring contrast between God's chosen people being generous and blessed with the inheritance of the land[2] and the wicked and the cursed, who cut themselves off from God's provision and generous blessings.

Consequences

Those who aren't openhanded are called wicked. They live with a posture of scarcity. Scarcity breeds envy, jealousy, and anxiety. Other people become competition or threats in the chase after power, position, or wealth.[3] The wicked look to these things to provide a false sense of stability and security. And this posture of idolatry is what separates the wicked from God. David explains that those who are cursed are cut off (Ps 37:22). Worse than suffering material need, those who are cut off from God truly have nothing. "What does it profit a man to gain the whole world and forfeit his soul?" (Mark 8:36 ESV). Being cut off from the God of the universe is being restricted from all his provision and blessing and, most importantly, his very presence and a life with him.

David writes a similar statement earlier in this psalm, "For the evildoers shall be cut off, but those who wait for the LORD shall inherit the land" (v. 9 ESV), reinforcing the same idea of the cursed not receiving an inheritance of the land. The Israelites understood the blessing of the land as having a place to dwell securely where they would enjoy Yahweh's blessing. The true safety and security of our lives come only in the Lord's presence, and David pens these contrasts so we see, clearly, the consequences of our decisions.

Hands: Clenched or Open?

I've counseled emerging ethnic leaders about the burrito situation. Often, they find themselves "taking one for the team" in work or ministry situations but feel frustrated and taken advantage of when others don't reciprocate or operate with the value of the collective. Sometimes these young leaders are asked to share painful personal stories and experiences of racism as a teaching point for the benefit of the majority culture. Often, they agree to share, especially if asked by someone who holds a leadership position or is older or more experienced (honoring our elders is an Eastern cultural value), but when their vulnerability is not reciprocated or shared in a safe space, they leave feeling exposed and used. Having found myself in those situations in the past, I now recommend practicing agency, and I now understand that it is perfectly fine to say no. Sharing our burrito in an environment that doesn't recognize the value of the collective can lead to burnout and cynicism. Instead, I inform young ethnic leaders that it is their choice whether they offer their knowledge, experience, extra hours, etc., as gifts with the full understanding that their offering may not be reciprocated.

I encourage you, sisters, as we go about our days, to recognize the beauty and God-honoring cultural values infused in our collective approach to living. We are always looking to honor those who have gone before us, to link arms with those around us, and to do what we can to help the next generation go further. We are presented with opportunities to generously serve as conduits of God's overflowing abundance. We serve the God who provided for the widow of Zarephath. He did not allow her flour to run out or her oil to run dry. And at the right time, God provided rain to end the famine. We, too, can trust God with our provisions, the wisdom to serve hospitably, and the stewardship of our resources. We, too, can be generous like our God.

For from him and through him and to him are all things. To him be glory forever. Amen. (Rom. 11:36 ESV)

Father, help us to remember and recognize that you are the generous giver of all. Everything belongs to you. All we have is from you. Your resources are unlimited, and you faithfully provide for generation after generation. Lead and guide us to the places where we can be conduits of your blessings to others. Strengthen us to practice living in abundance instead of scarcity. Expand our hearts. May our lives and the blessings you've provided replenish those in need around us. Amen.

Dr. Mabel Ping-Hua Lee (1896–1966)

Giving without Getting

One of the most challenging parts of living with generosity is the reality that we may not get to see and enjoy the outcome of our investments and service. Dr. Mabel Ping-Hua Lee is a historical trailblazer who lived this reality. She was the first Chinese woman in the United States to earn a PhD in economics, which she earned from Columbia University in 1921.

While she celebrated several individual wins, many injustices remained for her people. The Chinese Exclusion Act of 1882 was the first and only law banning a specific ethnic or national group from immigrating to the United States.[4] Lee's father served as a Chinese missionary and pastor of the Baptist Chinese Mission in New York's Chinatown. Both her parents, Lee Towe and Lee Lai Beck, were teachers in the Baptist church, and for that reason, they were among the few Chinese who were exempt from the act, allowing them to become immigrants, though they were never granted citizenship. When Lee was nine years old, she immigrated with the rest of her family to New York from Guangzhou, China, to join her father (who had arrived in the US a few years earlier).

Despite the racist injustice and invisibility at the beginning of her journey, Lee is remembered as a leader in the suffrage movement in New York.[5] She was at the forefront of the women's suffrage movement. At the age of sixteen, she led thousands of women on horseback into the streets of New York to advocate for their rights even though the Chinese Exclusion Act prevented her from voting. Lee attended the all-female counterpart to Columbia, Barnard College, and majored in history and philosophy. There she continued to work for equal voting rights for women. She also wrote feminist essays for the college newspaper, gave speeches on voting rights, and was a leader in the Chinese Students' Alliance of the United States of America. Lee was passionate about the involvement and education of Chinese American women of all ages. She considered women "the Submerged Half,"[6] and the basic civil rights of women, especially Chinese American women, kept her at the forefront of addressing injustice. In 1917, women in New York State were granted the right to vote. The Nineteenth Amendment passed in 1920, granting white women the right to vote throughout the nation. Twenty-five years later, women of Chinese descent finally received the right to vote after the repeal of the Chinese Exclusion Act in 1943. Researchers and historians are unsure if Lee ever attained citizenship and her right to vote, but her leadership and legacy paved the way for future generations to exercise the privilege of voting.

Even though the laws remained unjust, Lee worked tirelessly for a brighter future for the next generation. She received her master's degree in educational administration at Barnard. She excelled as a leader and a scholar. While working on her doctorate in economics at Columbia University, she was the first Chinese student to receive the University Scholar in Economics award.

When she was twenty-eight, the sudden death of her father led her to become the director of the Baptist Chinese Mission. She raised funds to purchase property for First Chinese Baptist Church. Lee believed in the importance of Chinese Christianity. The European American Protestantism, which focused primarily on "individual salvation" and "a personal relationship with God," didn't capture what her collective culture taught. She followed in her father's footsteps in pursuing a more progressive social gospel that intentionally set out to invest in the local Chinatown community. This expression of faith that embraced collective flourishing and community involvement matched her scriptural belief about what it meant to live as a Christian. Under her leadership, the church became the first self-supporting Chinese church in America. And the church still stands today, offering the same services of English classes, kindergarten, vocational training, and health clinics for the Chinese immigrant community.[7] Recently, a post office in downtown Chinatown was named after Lee to honor her contribution, leadership, and dedication to the people and local community. Lee's testimony inspires us to continue giving even if our life's work is not fully realized in our lifetime, but each of us can trust that God's purposes and plans will prevail as we walk in step with the Spirit.

STROPHE 5

PSALM 37:23–28a

SEVENTEEN

Este Mvskokvlke, paksvnke, mucvnettv, pakse

Mvskoke People, Yesterday, Today, Tomorrow

A Liturgy by Mariah Humphries, Mvskoke Nation Citizen

> God of the removed generations,
> we are yours.

> (Mvskoke/Muscogee "Creek")
> Cehofvt este-hunvnwv ele vwiketvn yekcicet os,
> momet em vyetvn es afvcket os.
> Latke estomis, tvkwihoke mahet omekares,
> Cehofvt e'nken hvlatet ok.
>
> Esvkvsvmkv 37:23–24

> Our steps are made firm by the LORD,
>   when he delights in our way;
> though we stumble, we shall not fall headlong,
>   for the LORD holds us by the hand.
>
> Psalm 37:23–24 NRSV

> With gentle breath, you formed us to reflect your image—
> and saw that we were good.

Through your reflection we are seen and loved by you. You made us with worth and purpose, to glorify your name. From the depth of generational oppression, we hold tightly to hope—you, Creator, Restorer, Mystery.

When we are removed, when we are disregarded, you whisper *I am with you* as a reminder that we know to whom we are cherished and uplifted.

By your stabilizing hand, you keep our heads raised and our eyes fixed on you—

> and we see who we are.
> We are not poverty, to you.
> We are not addiction, to you.
> We are not retained to the past, to you.
> We are not sanitized history, to you.
> We are not a societal burden, to you.
> Our culture is not mocked by you.
> You see us as your creation and by you we are strengthened.
> *We are imago Dei, made in your image.*
> Our wailing has long been expressed, yet we know you are there,
> in your divine timeline, listening.
> We feel you moving, Yahweh.

This land is witnessing the awakening of the original children, and you are revealing the Native voice that has long been suppressed. God, let our wailing overwhelm all oppression and suppression. Let the inhabitants of the land know we belong to you.

Our souls yearn for you in our troubled days, and our hearts long for justice to be claimed.

You alone are the hands of justice, the obtainer of Truth.

> God of the invisible, make us seen.

With each step taken by our Mvskoke mothers and daughters over unfamiliar hills and mountains, you were our inner shelter against the plague of conquest. With every death, you mourned with us. We were wounded but not obsolete. You held back the genocidal hand in order for the surviving generations to pass down culture and language.

> Our culture represents your diverse beauty.
> Our language is your language. We are understood by you.

We are crying out, "How long must we stumble? How long must we suffer? Where is the hand of deliverance, the embrace of restoration?" Yahweh, we are weary. But you are not bound to our limited strength or our shortsightedness.

Renew our patience and willfulness so we may be steadfast for the journey ahead.

> As clarity fades, your promise is our guide.
> As our hope falters, our place in your story is our light.

> **With Yahweh, we are not invisible.**
> Cv mvnette arvyvtet, momet hiyomat vc vculet os,
> momis este faccvn wihoken hecvkot, en honvpset tvklike
>   vpohaken hccvkates.
> Estofis est en heromet,
> est em palet os: momen en honvpsen ohmerkvt oh ocet os.

> I have been young, and now am old,
> yet I have not seen the righteous forsaken
>   or their children begging bread.
> They are ever giving liberally and lending,
> and their children become a blessing. (Psalm 37:25–26
>   NRSV)

We have witnessed the terminal pain from elders before us. We plead with you to protect us from the same pain of being silenced.

Lead us away from accepting a foreign culture as our purpose, and remind us we are your people, and yours alone.

May our communal heritage flow through our children and their children's children. May we never disappear as victims of genocidal sin.

From the young with passion, to the old with wisdom, bless our generations.

You created us for connection—to one another and to the land and sea. May we feel the presence of you with every touch of the earth you provide. May your intimacy be received in the gentleness of the breeze, and may we know your power in the strength of the wind. Revive us with baptism in our ancestral waters.

Keep our souls on the eternal, in the midst of present turmoil. Let us recognize our worth in a world of temporal acknowledgment and success.

Our generations are suffering from an internal wound that will not heal on its own. Our matriarchal ancestors were removed from the land, from families, from culture, and from language, and forced into violent conditions with the purpose to *kill the Indian and save the man*, as was the battle cry of the oppressor.

Yahweh, Native women and girls in our lifetime are suffering the same violence as our ancestors. We are stolen, we are missing, we are murdered,[1] and we are wailing for our sisters, but the cries fall upon deaf ears. Project our cries, Lord, and open the ears of others.

We know you sit with our women and girls in unknown locations and hold them as they tremble. For those who do not return in this life, may you be the presence they feel, and may they know they are not lost, for you are there.

With Yahweh, we are not missing.
Holwakan enkvpaket, heren momecvs;
momet estofis liketskvres.

151

Cehofvt fvcceckvn vnokecet, em vnokeckakan wike kot
    omekv;
meyuksv-sekon vcayecvkhoyet os.

Depart from evil, and do good;
    so you shall abide forever.
For the LORD loves justice;
        he will not forsake his faithful ones. (Psalm 37:27–28
        NRSV)

Only by your carefully crafted plan can we obtain justice.

Our bodies may exist in invisibility for a moment, but we rest in knowing we are not forsaken by you. We were once removed but anticipate the first steps on our eternal, promised, ancestral land.

You handcrafted our seat at your table of justice. Keep us from engaging in divisiveness with other relatives—our Black, Asian, and Latina sisters. Whether through judgment of the color of our skin, economic diversity, or comparing our pain and depth of wounds, conduct our voices in a chorus of unity in pursuit of justice and equity. May we remember you made each of us for your purpose.

When others suppress our volume, bring to mind how you handcrafted our seat at your table of justice—a position of confidence that reminds us:

We are seen,
We are heard,
We are uplifted.

May our wailing rattle the bones of the sustainers of our oppression. May their reliance on the foundation of superiority be shattered under your feet.

Indigenize our land's history, our present, our future. Give our people redemption and heal our Trail of Tears.

Este Mvskokvlke paksvnke, mucvnettv, pakse.
Mvskoke people, yesterday, today, tomorrow.

With Yahweh, we are not forsaken.

Mariah Humphries (MTS) is a Mvskoke Nation citizen, writer, and educator. Through her experience navigating the tension between Native and white American culture, she brings Native awareness to non-Native spaces. With over twenty years of vocational ministry service, she is focused on theology, racial literacy, and reconciliation within the American church.

With YAHWEH,
I AM not invisible.
I AM not missing.
I AM not forsaken!

EIGHTEEN

Though We Stumble

The LORD makes firm the steps
   of the one who delights in him;
though he may stumble, he will not fall,
   for the LORD upholds us with his hand.

Psalm 37:23–24

Sheila Wise Rowe (MEd) is a truth-teller, passionate about faith, emotional and racial trauma healing, and (re)conciliation. She advocates for the dignity and rights of the marginalized and abused. For thirty years Sheila was a therapist in Boston, France, and South Africa, and is now a sought-after writer, speaker, and spiritual director. She authored *Healing Racial Trauma* and *Young, Gifted, and Black: A Journey of Lament and Celebration*.

B lack women are all too familiar with grief. We push it down so we can carry on, but there's a high cost. Our bodies remember. Emotionally, we carry the lash marks and the words that sought to crush and break our spirits. Left behind are the wounds of racial trauma: we weep in silence; we pray in silence. Our paths are littered with rocks, hurdles, and barriers that cause us to stumble. Sometimes we stumble over our own sin, but here we lament, for racism has transmuted into a multitude of state-sanctioned stumbling blocks. They are placed in

155

our way to impede our forward movement. Yet, we persevere while unseen and unheard. We press on, determined to reach Jesus even as the stumbling blocks mount.

I'm reminded of the story in John 11. Sisters Mary and Martha send word to Jesus that their brother, Lazarus, is ill. When Jesus learns his friends are in distress, he says he intends to go to them, although the last time he was in town, the Jewish leaders wanted to stone him. The disciples caution Jesus, who then responds, "Are there not twelve hours of daylight? Anyone who walks in the daytime will not stumble, for they see by this world's light. It is when a person walks at night that they stumble, for they have no light" (v. 9). I believe Jesus is saying that even when it's dark or bleak, the light will keep us from stumbling and falling headlong into despair. In situations like this, Jesus embodies the light. He is Emmanuel, God with us.

Meanwhile, Jesus delays going to the sisters. Mary and Martha thought they knew how it would all go down. Jesus would miraculously appear just in time to heal Lazarus. But he does not. Lazarus dies, darkness falls, and the sisters stumble.

Eventually, we all have moments like this; no longer waiting women, we become wailing women. Our grief is beyond bearing, and it seems that Jesus is nowhere to be found. I had such a moment when I watched the video of George Floyd's murder by the police.[1] In the last moments of his life, he cried, "Momma! Momma! I'm through."

Lonnae O'Neal wrote, "I recognize his words. A call to your mother is a prayer to be seen. Floyd's mother died two years prior, but he used her as a sacred invocation. . . . To call out to his mother is to be known to his maker. The one who gave him to her."[2]

As I watched the video, I became a wailing woman and mother. I was crying out for this son and father, now dead, and his beloved momma. I prayed and pleaded for George to be seen, for Black people to be seen.

I wonder if Mary and Martha questioned their relationship with Jesus. Did he really see, know, love, and value them as was reported? If so, why was he taking so long? By the time Jesus arrives, Lazarus has been in the tomb for four days. Martha goes out to meet Jesus, but Mary stays at home.

Remember in Luke 10:38–42, when Mary chose to be with Jesus, to sit at the Lord's feet, listening to what he said? Meanwhile, Martha was all about the work and complained to Jesus, "Tell her to help me!"

"'Martha, Martha,' the Lord answered, 'you are worried and upset about many things, but few things are needed—or indeed only one. Mary has chosen what is better, and it will not be taken away from her'" (vv. 40–41). But in John 11:21–23, it is Martha's faith that we see as we read:

> "Lord," Martha said to Jesus, "if you had been here, my brother would not have died. But I know that even now God will give you whatever you ask."
>
> Jesus said to her, "Your brother will rise again."

Mary stays home, disappointed and in so much pain that it is hard for her to delight herself in the Lord. Like Mary, we too stumble and do not always rush out to meet with or welcome Jesus. Martha returns home and tells Mary, "The Teacher is here . . . and is asking for you" (v. 28). When Mary hears this, she gets up quickly and goes to Jesus. She falls at his feet and says, "Lord, if you had been here, my brother would not have died" (v. 32).

Then we read the shortest sentence in all of Scripture: "Jesus wept" (v. 35). The fact that he wept is profound because Jesus knew that he'd soon raise Lazarus from the dead. Yet, he sobbed over the pain of the sisters and the momentary loss of his dear friend. In moments like this, amid our horror and devastation, we are assured that Jesus sees us, hears us, and acknowledges the depth of our pain and grief.

Psalm 37 reminds us that the Lord makes firm the steps of the one wailing woman who delights in him; though we may stumble, we will not fall, for the Lord upholds us with his hand. Jesus upholds these two sisters and calls forth Lazarus from the grave, just like he calls other folks and things to life.

When Jesus tells the family and community to remove the grave-clothes that still have Lazarus bound, there is a collective effort to completely free him. In the same way, we need the Lord and each other to help remove the stumbling blocks and the things that still have us and the next generation bound. Hebrews 12:12–13 encourages us in the Lord to "take a new grip with [our] tired hands, stand firm on [our] shaky legs, and mark out a straight, smooth path for [our] feet so that those who follow [us], though weak and lame, will not fall and hurt themselves but become strong" (TLB).

Lord, you are Emmanuel, God with us. You weep with us and offer love and comfort in our distress. You resurrect and redeem all that has been lost or stolen. Because you uphold us, we can "throw off everything that hinders and the sin that so easily entangles. And . . . run with perseverance the race marked out for us, fixing our eyes on Jesus, the pioneer and perfecter of faith. For the joy set before him [Jesus] endured the cross, scorning its shame, and sat down at the right hand of the throne of God. [Help us] to consider him who endured such opposition from sinners, so that [we] will not grow weary and lose heart" (Heb. 12:1–3). In Jesus's name. Amen.

Dr. Rebecca Lee Crumpler (1831–95)

A Life Prayerfully Offered

Dr. Rebecca Lee Crumpler, born in Delaware to Absolum Davis and Matilda Webber, was raised by an aunt in Pennsylvania. In 1852, Rebecca began her seven-year career as a nurse in Boston, Massachusetts, while aspiring to become a doctor. This seemed unlikely because there were few Black doctors among the fifty-four thousand in America, and none of them were women. The New England Female Medical College in Boston faced ongoing backlash for training women. In 1860, when the country was on the verge of civil war, it was scandalous to enroll Black women in the medical college; however, Rebecca was admitted. This is a testament to her intellect, skills as a nurse, and the glowing references received from white male physicians. Rebecca's tuition was covered by the Wade Scholarship Fund created by the Ohio abolitionist Benjamin Wade. Like the other female medical students, she faced obstacles.[3] Despite these stumbling blocks, Dr. Rebecca Lee Crumpler graduated in 1864 as the first and only African American graduate from the medical school and the first Black female doctor in America.

Dr. Crumpler had a deep faith. She delighted in the Lord and took direction from him. She had a loving family and a thriving medical practice, but she heeded the call to go to post–Civil War Richmond, Virginia. There she worked with the Freedmen's Bureau to offer medical care to over ten thousand formerly enslaved. She wrote that Virginia was "a proper field for real missionary work, and one that would present ample opportunities to become acquainted with the diseases of women and children."[4] Dr. Crumpler set up a tent hospital but was faced with a lack of doctors, nurses, and medical supplies.

As she worked at the Bureau, reports indicate that "hospitals would not admit her patients; druggists would not fill her prescriptions or sell her supplies."[5] She had to petition her medical college to donate medicine and bandages.[6] Dr. Crumpler stumbled and could have fallen after contracting typhoid and malaria. She could have given up and gone home, but she persevered and for five years offered exceptional medical and spiritual care.

When she returned to Boston, she opened a medical practice that served women and children. In 1883, she wrote the first medical book written by an African American, *A Book of Medical Discourses in Two Parts*, about her obstetrics and pediatrics experience.[7] She is found in history books, her house is on the Boston Women's Heritage Trail, and a scholarship fund and an organization that supports Black women physicians bear her name. However, for 125 years, she lay buried in an unmarked grave.

In February 2020, the Friends of the Hyde Park Library discovered this and raised funds for a proper headstone. On July 16, 2020, during the COVID-19 pandemic, they held a socially distanced celebration of the tombstone unveiling. During Dr. Crumpler's lifetime, the Lord upheld her with his hand, and even 125 years after her death, this phenomenal woman is seen and honored. Dr. Crumpler wrote the following dedication in her book: "To mothers and nurses and all who may desire to mitigate the afflictions of the human race, this book is prayerfully offered."[8] Those words could be a motto for how she overcame stumbling blocks, lived, and served. Hers was a life prayerfully offered. May it be the same for each of us.

NINETEEN

Hunger Pains

I was young and now I am old,
    yet I have never seen the righteous forsaken
    or their children begging bread.
They are always generous and lend freely;
    their children will be a blessing.

Psalm 37:25–26

QuaWanna N. Bannarbie is an African American writer and teacher who was born and raised in historic Americus, Georgia. She contributes weekly to the *Suffolk News-Herald*, the newspaper of Suffolk, Virginia. She is a founding director for the nonprofit Leadership LINKS, Inc., and instructs at Indiana Wesleyan University. She and her husband, Tyrone, have three children.

Psalm 37:25 begins like a storyteller starts a fable: "I was young and now I am old . . ." Storytelling is an ancient craft that helps hearers to visualize, commit, and learn the lessons. There is a lesson about the goodness of God and his spiritual and physical provision for you today. A seasoned person pays attention to instruction to incline their heart toward God, so they can give generously and lend freely, and so their own children can learn the same and be a blessing.

A Bowl of Goodness

Can you remember the last time you were really hungry? Scientists who have studied nutrition and the digestive system believe that the purpose of hunger is to remind us that our bodies need to be fueled to sustain optimal operation.[1] A prolonged empty stomach due to food poverty causes hunger pangs, which is the body's painful way of begging. God designed our bodies to feel and recognize this pain, and no one wants to bear witness to this pain in the lives of children.

When I was growing up, missions campaigns and television infomercials conditioned us to imagine hunger through the large eyes of poor children across the globe. Their eyes were filled with tears. Their lips, the color of ash, were badly cracked. Their brown skin was tight to their bones. The camera panned out to reveal the rest of their bodies. Empty bowls sat between their skeletal-looking legs. Then someone walked over with a long ladle and poured a runny, white, grain-like substance into their bowls. A nearby woman, maybe a mother or a surviving relative who cared for them, scooped some into her hands and then to their mouths. These vittles may not have looked like much, but it stopped the tears of women and children who were wasting away, pierced with the pains of hunger.

The pain of not being able to feed children can be known to any woman, whether she is a mother, grandmother, daughter, auntie, widow, sister, or barren friend. Women around the world bear the responsibility of food acquisition and preparation. Filling empty bowls is a heavy duty.

Soup for the Soul

Black people have made a name for the bowls of their cuisine. The term "soul food" is loosely related to the rations given to control the enslaved Africans in the southern United States of America. Slave masters provided minimal nutrition to support the dietary energy needed for slave labor.[2] An allotment of a peck of cornmeal and pork rinds became the elemental components for my enslaved ancestors' remedy for hunger.[3] They supplemented meager rations with their African heritage to innovate and influence American culture and cuisine.[4]

For generations, Black women have nursed survival with their own hands. That generational transfer of nurturing Black families with few resources created cuisine such as Hoppin' John with black-eyed peas and collard greens, stewed tomatoes and okra, spoonbread, or shrimp and grits. Soul food recipes are history and legacy for the women in my family. My great-grandmother, Ruby "Jane" Harris, the wife of Alfred "Perry" Harris—a sharecropper who worked for a white farmer who frequently denied him equitable pay for his labor—taught my grandmother, Fannie, how to stretch portions, enliven poor-quality meats, and grow fresh vegetables to supplement her family's diet. Fannie passed that on to my mother, Frances.

Long before Jack Canfield and Mark Victor Hansen created their book series Chicken Soup for the Soul, my mother's warm, comforting bowls of vegetable soup relieved our growling stomachs. While not a popular soul food recipe, scraps became scrumptious soup in my momma's hands. Sometimes she saved turkey and ham bones in the freezer to create broth for another delectable goulash. She never wasted the remaining juices from a pot of greens. When times became hard, and they did, her pot liquor was just as good as any bouillon base. Chowder was not reserved for winter months; Momma made soup any time of the year. I didn't understand why soup was my mother's go-to meal until I became a mother.

My parents separated in 1981. I was just entering kindergarten, one of my sisters was four years old, and my youngest sister was a newborn baby. Momma stretched her dollars from paycheck to paycheck using portion control and preparing one-pot meals. We may have had little. Yet, we did not starve. The faces of hungry children resembled my brown skin, *but* because of my mother, I was not one of them.

My maternal great-grandparents struggled to feed their fourteen children. My grandmother Fannie is the third oldest. When she reads the words of the psalmist, she says, "That's us!" She testifies that "they never went hungry even if a meal was simply a buttered biscuit and homemade syrup." Four generations of women—Ruby, Fannie, Frances, and now me—can testify to the truth of Psalm 37:25–26. Despite divorce, we were not forsaken. Despite our painful history of slave rations, we were not forsaken. Despite overwork and under-payment, we were not forsaken. God has never forsaken us! He has made physical and spiritual provisions throughout our generations. My inheritance is a strong history of faith within our family, which fuels my soul and equips my hands to fill the prayer bowls of heaven (Rev. 5:8) as I freely lend my service to community, church, and family.

Soul and Substance

The words *soul* and *soup* differ by only one letter. Hunger can be the malnutrition of our stomachs and our souls. God created us to identify hunger pains so that our spiritual intercession and physical interven-tion on behalf of the poor, hungry, and needy may inspire our appetite to become the hands of God. Like nursing mothers, we can introduce children to spiritual food whether they are heirs biologically or spiritu-ally. We can cultivate this sacred relationship with the Bread of Life, Jesus Christ, knowing that he beckons children to come to him and he promises that those who come "will never go hungry" (John 6:35). It's a blessing to know that "the LORD does not let the righteous go hungry, but he thwarts the craving of the wicked" (Prov. 10:3).

The Bread of Life Is Sufficient

If you are an expectant mother, your child can hear your voice singing hymns of praise in the womb. If you are a children's ministry leader, you have the precious time to familiarize schoolchildren with the Bread of Life by reading Bible stories to them. If you have no children at all, you have a testimony to share of your personal relationship with Christ.

Never neglect to recall your faith journey and the historical narrative of the faith of your family. Be like the psalmist—a storyteller: "I was young and now I am old . . ." Like an old Black grandmother, Madea, or matriarch, the writer invites us to climb into their lap, or sit around the kitchen table, and train our ears again to hear a story about the Bread of Life. As you read the Word with young disciples, you are conditioning their hearts to break bread together and honor what God has asked us to do as often as we proclaim the Lord Jesus until he returns (1 Cor. 11:24–25). Spirit-filled women of God can ladle heaps of spiritual "food" and "drink" to share with the next generation. "For he satisfies the thirsty and fills the hungry with good things" (Ps. 107:9). The Word of God is a meal. Our soul provider really satisfies.

Dear Jesus, the children are hungry and crying for bread (Lam. 4:4). Your Word says, "Yet have I never seen the righteous forsaken" (Ps. 37:25). Stir up the righteous who remedy the meager offerings of this world with indulgence in a life satisfied by an all-sufficient God. Guide the children to follow your recipe to become your disciples and willingly love the Lord their God with all their heart, and with all their soul, and with all their mind (Matt. 23:37). Thank you that your love remedies our hunger so that we have no need to beg. In Jesus's name. Amen.

Patreece Lewis

"I AIN'T AFRAID OF YOUR JAIL"

The Leesburg Stockade Girls

Children Hungry for Justice

Whatever we feed our children—natural food or exposure to new environments—will affect their growth. History demonstrates that many inspiring justice seekers and freedom fighters were introduced to their faith journey at an early age. The mentors and caregivers in their community taught them to prove God's Word in their own lives.

My father's first cousin, Sandra Mansfield, was the youngest of the stolen Black girls of the Leesburg Stockade, who were imprisoned for peaceful protests against segregation in 1963.[5] She joined the Civil Rights Movement at twelve years of age.

In 1963, Americus, Georgia, was a hotseat of racial prejudice and seditious crimes against the Black community. Following the arrest of Dr. Martin Luther King Jr. for his efforts to desegregate public facilities in the city of Albany, Georgia, the movement shifted to Americus and its headquarters at Allen Chapel African Methodist Episcopal (AME) Church.[6] The Student Nonviolent Coordinating Committee (SNCC) planned a protest march for Blacks to buy tickets to attend the local theater. Fifteen Black girls aged twelve to fifteen joined over two hundred people to march from Friendship Baptist Church to Martin Theatre.[7] The girls refused to disperse and were taken from the protest. Because the local jail was full of adult protestors, they were taken to an old stockade in Leesburg, Georgia. Their parents had no idea where they were for forty-five days.

These girls became teachers and leaders in my community. Emmarene Kaigler Streeter, another "stolen girl," was my guidance counselor for my first two years of high school. Allen Chapel AME Church is the home church of my youth. These women served as witnesses to us of what it means to raise children to believe the Word of the Lord. They were young but still stood tall as loyal, brave, and true figures of justice who believed the Lord for deliverance from the oppression of the Jim Crow South. They remind me of the monument in Kelly Ingram Park in Birmingham, Alabama, that is inscribed with the words *I ain't afraid of your jail.*

According to historical accounts, articles, records, and interviews given by the women, who are now over sixty years old or deceased, they spent many days of their imprisonment with little to no sustenance, but their spiritual bellies were not empty. Like Paul and Silas, they sang songs of deliverance and believed that God heard. God did not forsake them.

The unjust imprisonment of these girls was intended to persuade their parents to silence, but their cries for justice revealed that they were a spiritually hungry bunch. Just as hunger pains bring awareness to the body of a need, the cries of these hungry youth brought awareness to the need for justice and change in Americus. Photos of the girls in captivity were published by SNCC and gained the attention of the nation. On September 15, 1963, law enforcement released the Leesburg Stockade Girls and returned them to their families.[8] This was the same week that four little girls—Addie Mae Collins (14), Denise McNair (14), Carole Robertson (14), and Cynthia Wesley (11)—were murdered by a racialized bombing at 16th Street Baptist Church in Birmingham, Alabama.[9] The story of the Leesburg Stockade Girls is just one of many testimonies of children who engaged in the fight for civil rights in our nation. Their spiritual rumblings and the generous sacrifice in their fight for freedom and integration have blessed us all.

THE LEESBURG STOCKADE GIRLS

Annie Lou Ragans Laster
Billie Jo Thornton Allen
Dr. Carol Barner-Seay
Diane Dorsey-Bowens
Emmarene Kaigler Streeter
Gloria Westbrooks Breedlove
Laura Ruff Saunders
Lulu Westbrooks Griffin
Mattie Crittenden
Melinda Jones Williams
Pearl Brown
Sandra Russell Mansfield
Dr. Shirley Green-Reese
Verna Hollis
Willie Mae Smith-Davis

TWENTY

The Lord Loves Justice

Turn away from evil and do good;
   so shall you dwell forever.
For the LORD loves justice;
   he will not forsake his saints.
They are preserved forever.

Psalm 37:27–28a ESV

Kristie Anyabwile is an African American author and editor of *His Testimonies, My Heritage: Women of Color on the Word of God*. She is the associate director of women's workshops at the Charles Simeon Trust. She is also a founding member of the Pelican Project. She disciples and teaches women at Anacostia River Church in Washington, DC, where her husband is senior pastor. They have three children.

As I watch my teenage son tower over me, his voice deepening into a Barry White–like baritone, I know I need to have "the talk" with him. I don't mean the sex talk. I mean the talk that Black and Brown families know all too well and dread with all their being. This is the talk that we hope and pray will keep our children alive if they have a negative encounter with police. As my young adult daughters drive around more independently and for longer distances, sometimes on barren stretches of the highway, I know I need to have "the talk" with them as well. I hate that we live in a society where uniformed officers, the ones my children understood to be community helpers as they were growing up, might be the very ones who stop and question them without due cause, and from whom they might need protection.

As a Christian, I find that it's an even more daunting task, because I also want to frame "the talk" from a faith perspective, to help them think and act safely, but also to help them think and act Christianly. But what do I say? How do I have the talk wisely? What do I tell them about the world and their place in it? What do I tell them about God and his response to evil and injustice? What do I tell them that would help in the moment of what could be a life-or-death encounter with the police? These verses in Psalm 37 are a great starting point.

We have learned that the righteous should be trusting and waiting patiently on the Lord to act in his righteousness toward the wicked. This entire psalm is written as proverbial instructions, like from a father to a son. I imagine David sitting young Solomon down as a teen, encouraging him not to burn with anger when he observes wickedness around him (vv. 1, 8) because one day "the wicked will perish" (v. 20). It's a coming-of-age psalm similar to Proverbs 1–7, where Solomon takes great pains to instruct his son in the way of wisdom, just as his father, David, did to him. It makes sense, then, that this psalm of David, full of instructional wisdom about the righteous and the wicked, gives us a blueprint of how to have "the talk" with our children.

Your Posture

We know from the tragic deaths of Black men like Philando Castile and Jonathan Price that the most compliant posture is no guarantee of safety. However, the instruction to "turn away from evil and do good" (Ps. 37:27) is a moral imperative that teaches us how we are to live before God and others. We are "created in Christ Jesus for good works, which God prepared beforehand, that we should walk in them" (Eph. 2:10 ESV). The good we do in the world is a demonstration of our faith in Christ (James 2:18), so it follows that those who have repented of their sin and turned away from evil to do the good works God has prepared for them will eternally dwell with God in his kingdom. The corresponding promise "so shall you dwell forever" of Psalm 37:27 assures us of our eternal inheritance. No matter what happens in this life, with both hands securely on the steering wheel, my children can rest in the security of knowing that they are kept by God, now and throughout eternity.

Your God

Both parent and child learn that right instructions and right actions provide no real guarantee of safety, yet they do promote neighborly love, and they show that we are committed to following the Lord in obedience to his commands. You can almost hear a child's response when the parent says, "Look, the first thing you need to do is turn away from evil and do good." Immediately, almost any child would raise a question about fairness. "What if I'm not being treated well? Why should I be good to someone who may not be good to me? How are my right actions going to help when evil is being imposed upon me?"

The next verse answers these potential objections with surprising clarity. We are to turn away from evil and do good because the Lord loves justice. Justice is more than the consequences that result from doing wrong (retributive justice). It is also restorative. Biblical justice highly values every person as made in the image of God; it seeks to reorient the trajectory of those who commit unjust acts to restore them to a right relationship with God and neighbor. Biblical justice considers the plight of the vulnerable and actively works to care for them and change societal structures that would otherwise keep them at a disadvantage.

This is the kind of justice that God loves. He cares way more about justice than you or I ever will. He doesn't merely act justly. He loves justice (Ps. 99:4; Isa. 61:8). The foundation of his throne is justice (Pss. 89:14; 97:2). His throne is established for justice, and it is from his throne that he judges righteously (Ps. 9:7–8). All of his ways are just. Moses declared it (Deut. 32:4), a pagan king acknowledged it (Dan. 4:37), and the angels sang of it (Rev. 15:3). Not only that, but he doesn't hide or hold back his justice; rather, he reveals his justice to his people (Ps. 37:6) and redeems his people by justice (Isa. 1:27). This biblical truth guards us from taking vengeance out on wrongdoers ourselves. If there is retribution to be made, God will enact it. If restoration is possible, the Lord will ensure it. God's love for justice also helps us to encourage our children in the truth that regardless of what happens in our moments of terror, we can trust God to act completely and decisively just.

God's Promise

We may not see his justice at work immediately or maybe even in our lifetime, but God will act on behalf of the righteous and will indeed judge the misdeeds of the wicked. And through it all, "he will not forsake his saints" (Ps. 37:28). He will be with us all the way. What a comfort to grieving mothers to know that God did not forsake Charleena Lyles, Sandra Bland, Atatiana Jefferson, or Breonna Taylor. He loves justice and will bring justice to those who have been pierced by the arrows of the wicked (v. 14). And for those who trust in Christ, "they are preserved forever" (v. 28). Death does not have the final say. As a matter of fact, death doesn't speak at all. Death is a responder. Christ speaks life eternal to the soul that leans on him for the rest that only he can give.

I can't guarantee safety for my children, but I can guarantee, based on these verses, that what Dr. Martin Luther King Jr. said is true: "when people get caught up with that which is right and they are willing to sacrifice for it, there is no stopping point short of victory."[1] Victory may look like driving away with a sigh of relief and with maybe a ticket in hand but limbs and life intact. Or, victory may look like entering glory and hearing the Lord's "well done" for turning away from evil and always seeking to do good out of love for God and neighbor.

There are two ways to view injustice in the world. We can continually look at the temporary prosperity of the wicked, asking why life is so unfair. Or we can look to the Lord, who teaches us how to live righteously in the world, who laughs in the face of wickedness—knowing that the day is coming when evil will get what it is due—who has prepared a perpetual dwelling for those who are his, and who loves justice so much that he sent his Son to die—the Just for the unjust—that he might bring us to God.

The Talk

So how will I have the talk with my children? I will direct them to follow the "Get Home Safely: 10 Rules of Survival."[2] More importantly, I will tell them to know who they are in Christ, to be the people whom God calls them to be in every circumstance, to turn from evil, to do good to everyone, and to leave their lives in the hands of Jesus, knowing that whatever the outcome, they will be with him and he will be with them. I will tell them that they can be sure that the Lord loves justice and that he will never leave them nor forsake them, especially in their time of need. They are kept safe forever with him.

> *Dear Jesus, we are grieved that we must have these conversations with our family. We lament injustice in all its forms and ask that you would restore our broken systems and strengthen our faith in you, as we remember your love for and commitment to justice. Let your justice roll down like a river, and righteousness like an ever-flowing stream (Amos 5:24). In Jesus's name. Amen.*

Harriet Jacobs (1813–97)

When Justice Is a Long Time Coming

Holed up in a crawl space in the roof of her grandmother's house for almost seven years, Harriet Jacobs prayed and planned for freedom for herself and her children. "I said to myself, 'Surely there must be some justice in man,' then I remembered, with a sigh, how slavery perverted all the natural feelings of the human heart."[3] The thin roof under which she lived provided little protection. She endured mice, mosquitoes, spring rain showers that drenched her makeshift bed and clothes, summer heat that dripped melted turpentine through the roof, and bitter cold winters that brought her close to death on several occasions. Harriet was cramped in a space where she could not stand or walk. She could see and hear her children and family enjoying life just below her but could not join them. She could not make a sound for hours on end, lest she be discovered and re-enslaved. Nevertheless, the years of silence and isolation and fear and pain were better than returning to a life of abuse and servitude.

Harriet Jacobs was born a slave in Edenton, North Carolina, and lived a happy childhood, unaware that she was a slave until her mother died. At six years old, Harriet took over her mother's duties as laborer for Margaret Horniblow, who treated her kindly and taught Harriet to read and write. However, things changed when Harriet turned twelve. Margaret died, and Harriet moved to the home of Dr. James and Mary Norcom. Harriet found no justice in this home. James was relentless in his sexual harassment of Harriet, and Mary was relentless in her jealous animosity toward Harriet. For ten years, Harriet suffered unimaginable abuse and trauma from the Norcom family, along with the atrocities she witnessed among family members, neighbors, and friends. When Harriet was fifteen years old, her true love interest was a free Black carpenter who wanted to marry her and purchase her freedom, but James Norcom forbade it. Responding in desperation, Harriet said, "I felt as if I was forsaken by God and man,"[4] so she engaged in a relationship with a white lawyer, Samuel Tredwell Sawyer, through whom she had two children.

Harriet found no justice in the promises of Samuel, who had assured her that he would emancipate his children. So, Harriet took it upon herself to fight for justice for herself and her children by running away from the Norcom home. She ended up in that attic crawl space for seven years, and eventually a plan was laid for her escape to New York. Though terrified, Harriet trudged through a snake-infested swamp to catch her boat to freedom, reasoning that "even those large, venomous snakes were less dreadful to my imagination than the white men in that community called civilized."[5]

Harriet's time in New York afforded her the opportunity to reunite with her brother John, who had escaped a few years prior, and to eventually make arrangements to reunite with her children, Joseph and Louisa Matilda. Yet, her pursuit of justice didn't stop there. Harriet published her autobiography to "arouse the women of the North to a realizing sense of the condition of two million of women [in] the South, still in bondage, suffering what I suffered, and most of them far worse. I want to add my testimony to that of abler pens to convince the people of the Free States what Slavery really is."[6]

Harriet was also active in the anti-slavery movement in New York. She started schools for freedmen in Alexandria, Virginia, and Savannah, Georgia, and she ran boardinghouses in Cambridge, Massachusetts, and Washington, DC, where she spent her final years.

For "A Change Is Gonna Come," singer-songwriter Sam Cooke included these lyrics: "It's been a long, a long time coming / But I know a change is gonna come, oh yes it will." Although it was "a long time coming" for Harriet to experience the freedom she deserved and longed for, and longer still to see systemic changes that would improve the trajectory for many African Americans, the story of Harriet's life is one that magnifies God's justice. He did not forsake her but preserved her for many good works, not only for this side of heaven but also for eternity. The inscription on her tombstone reflects her life well: "Patient in tribulation, fervent in spirit serving the Lord" (from Rom. 12:11–12).

STROPHE 6

PSALM 37:28b–33

TWENTY-ONE

The Peacemaker

With a Throat Full of Heart and Ancestors

A Poem by Carolina Hinojosa-Cisneros, Tejana, Chicana, and *Mujerista* Poet

Toward peace, an egress through lament, we
walked, sometimes marched, bodies upright,
spirits in our hands, throats full of heart and ancestors.

Toward the peacemaker's blessing, a bridge on fire, we
ran, sometimes marched, faced by the dawn ready
    for the morn,
hips full of curve, crested for the carrying.

Lament stitched into the hem of Sunday morning
    best, we
tugged at loose threads, unraveled at your wonder
    singing
working class hymns, twisting tongues into new
    language.

Blessed are those, and you wonder who? Are we
    those?
Because sometimes the fight is dirty—they don't live
    on these streets.
Sometimes the fight is lost—they don't work on
    these streets.

They say the wicked will pay, but we are all paying.
Customers
in a line paved in gold toward unrest, toward promised
freedom.
We've lost our best to diseases of the mind and body,
ancestors made too soon.

The promise of freedom doesn't lie on paved streets.
Freedom
comes from our relationship with our Maker—a dance
we choreograph together. In each motion, a rhythm
toward peace.

The making is an undoing with a throat full of heart and
ancestors.
When the making is a stone you fling at a giant, the
empire falls.
When the making is a song you pen in darkness, the sky
opens.

Toward the peacemaker's lot, a community in making, we
till new life, loosen the hardened earth within ourselves.
Hips crested, made ready for the water. Hands made
ready for the revival.

Carolina Hinojosa-Cisneros is a Tejana, Chicana, and *Mujerista* writer and poet from San Antonio, Texas. She is a member of the board of directors for Arts, Religion, Culture (ARC). In her work, Carolina explores storytelling, faith, and social justice.

TWENTY-TWO

Meekness, Not Weakness

Wrongdoers will be completely destroyed;
   the offspring of the wicked will perish.
The righteous will inherit the land
   and dwell in it forever.

Psalm 37:28b–29

Noemi Chavez has served as the lead pastor at Revive Church, a multisite in the greater Los Angeles area, for over fifteen years. She is the daughter of Mexican immigrants. Noemi is the co-founder of Brave Global, a nonprofit bridging collaboration of church and state to better serve girls on probation and in foster care. Noemi also serves as chair of the board for Exponential Español, a church-planting network.

Blessed are the meek, for they shall inherit the earth." That's Jesus's teaching from his Sermon on the Mount in Matthew 5:5. These are the words spoken by the living God, the mighty God who is not controlled by anger, disappointments, or wrath. Instead, he is the only one who committed to love selflessly by offering a perfect sacrifice that would cover a multitude of sins. This gracious gift is a blessing that the meek willingly receive. We receive it because we have been injured. We receive it because we are deficient. We receive it because we are not always strong, we cannot save ourselves, and we are fully dependent on the grace and justice of God.

True Inheritance of the Meek

Is it weak to be meek? Meekness is not the bowing of one's head in utter submission to injustice, nor is it the approval of the dehumanization of oneself or another. No! The meek are not ignorant of, unresponsive to, or unaffected by the plight of the world. In Christlikeness, the meek are those who are keenly aware of or "woke" to the pains of society. They are indignant, experiencing a rage and a fire in their hearts—and much like a dragon, they can exhale and burn down a city. For the meek, this impassioned anger is harnessed. They lord over it, making it submit to them. No weakness found here, friends. This submitted passion and righteous anger can turn into a pathway for justice movements, healing power, and third-day resurrections.

In his sermon, I do not believe that Jesus was talking about the real estate of precious lands in Jerusalem, prime locations near the Sea of Galilee, or rich soil in wine or olive country. Otherwise, he wouldn't be the God who came for the sick and the healthy, the poor and the wealthy, the Jew and the Gentile, the obscure and the prominent. The equity we gain through our relationship with Jesus, and the relationships that the church builds in the communities we inhabit, is far greater and more valuable than land, possessions, and physical territories. How beautiful is it that the righteous inherit this earth, all coming from the soil of relational spaces that make our lives here on God's earth richer?

Meekness stems from a soul rooted in Christ. Meekness at its core is self-control, wisdom, and influence, all of which when translated and leveraged into conversations can effectively introduce answers and solutions to systemic issues. In other words, our real estate is not only in the places we occupy but also in the atmospheres we create. The meek nonintrusively invite those within their circles of influence into a communal unity within diversity that can prove powerful and transformative to families, communities, villages, and cities. For the meek to inherit the earth, our communication must pierce through the layers of personal preference and create a vision for the future where everyone has a role to play. This practice can yield a powerful response that can spread like a California wildfire into the hearts of people, where the true treasures are found.

The Earth Is Ours

The meek will inherit the earth. There is no weakness in this inheritance. It comes from a long-suffering that translates into a voice, an answer, a movement that effects change in our communities. As followers of Jesus, we live between the reality of this world and the promises we hope for in the next. How reassuring it is knowing that the fire our Lord places in our bellies is not destructive to set a forest aflame but rather productive to blaze a healing path in the middle of our heartache and pain.

In 2013, the chief innovation officer in the city of Long Beach, California, informed me that over 80 percent of the girls being trafficked and trapped in the sex trade industry in our city grew up in the foster care system. Have you ever received information that made your heart feel like a heavy sandbag that sank into the pit of your stomach? Well, upon hearing this news, I felt righteous indignation filling my heart that could have driven me to burn down all the strip clubs and motels in my city. It's heartbreaking to have overwhelming evidence that the systems that are supposed to protect the most vulnerable are instead used to produce a brokenness where predators can introduce the enslavement of girls and women. In this instance, the blessedness of understanding our inheritance in Jesus led me down not a path of destruction but rather one of healing with my community. Meekness informed us what to do. We prayed and asked for God's favor. Prayer works and God's favor rests upon us when our mission is aligned with his heart.

Following prayer, our kingdom inheritance allowed us to use our earthly influence and authority to dive into the tension of church and state. We entered relationships to gain the trust of social workers, the bureau chief of probation, the school district representatives, and the city police, and together, we all got to work. The deep sorrow and the rage of injustice led by the Holy Spirit paved a pathway to bring freedom, knowledge, awareness, and empowerment to teenage girls in our city. Together, we learned that this life of meekness is rooted in a holy tension of living in the now-and-not-yet kingdom of God, and that yielding to the power of the Holy Spirit guarantees a fruitfulness that in time turns into shade, healing, and provision for others.

The Meek for the Wicked

Through our work at Brave Global, we have seen the sorrow and the deep disillusionment in the eyes of women and children who are victimized by their families and society. We all know what it looks like when the women and girls in our communities are consistently overlooked, underrepresented, or unsafe. God knows and sees this injustice in our lands too.

When the people of Israel were captives in Babylon, God gave them specific orders: "work for the peace and prosperity of the city where I sent you into exile. Pray to the LORD for it, for its welfare will determine your welfare" (Jer. 29:7). In the holy tension of their exile, God essentially said to his people, you are to work for peace and pray for your current city because their prosperity is connected to yours. So, I ask, "What is robbing people of peace in our world? Whose welfare has God tied to your welfare?" Our blessings and our peace are interconnected, and so is our destruction.

The visceral attacks in our communities must be stopped because they harm the righteous and the wicked alike.

The visceral attacks in our communities must be stopped because they harm the righteous and the wicked alike. Psalm 37:28 says, "The offspring of the wicked will perish." They are susceptible to certain death if the behavior of their parents is not corrected. Left to their own devices, they are prone to repeat the wicked actions of their heritage and therefore suffer the consequences. We don't want children to die; we want generational curses broken. That's why the meek must act in the face of injustice.

Lord, guard me from becoming numb to the wounds and the pain this world inflicts on others. Show me how I can take this bellyaching feeling and turn it into a solution in the lives of those who feel unseen and forgotten. Amen.

Comandante Ramona (1959–2006)

A Meek Revolutionary

There is no weakness in spiritual war and the fight for justice. I have known about the Zapatistas since I was in high school, but it wasn't until a few years ago that I learned of the courage of Comandante Ramona. The Zapatista Army of National Liberation, known in Mexico as EZLN, is a militant group whose initial roots emerged in the late 1960s but who evolved and officially organized as a revolutionary movement in 1994. They gained the attention of the Mexican government, the nation, and the world by demanding education equity, land rights, and improved living conditions for the Indigenous people of Chiapas, Mexico.

Comandante is Spanish for "commander." The year before the EZLN took its initial public stance, Comandante Ramona and other female commanders met with thousands of Indigenous women to create what would become known as the Women's Revolutionary Law, which was made public on January 1, 1994, the same day the Zapatista Army of National Liberation released their declaration to the Mexican government. Fighting for justice was her life. Comandante Ramona's commitment to this long and arduous movement was made more evident when she was diagnosed with cancer in the same year.

The laws she and her fellow commanders wrote provided women with the right to participate equally alongside men and earn military rank in the revolution. As a result, the women had the right to work, receive a fair salary, and decide how many children they would have. The women also had the right to become elected officials and serve in their community. They and their children would now receive primary care for their health and nutritional provision. They could choose whom to marry and live free of violence, and any acts against them (physical or sexual) would be severely punished. This is what happens when the meek become strong revolutionaries.

Comandante Ramona was known for her peaceful demeanor, but do not be misled; she was passionately committed to the revolution. She was the first Zapatista who was granted permission from the Mexican government to leave Chiapas and give peace talks. In her personal life and public advocacy, Comandante Ramona lived in the tension of what was and what could be. Despite the depletion of her health, her wise and unwavering commitment alongside the EZLN allowed them to gather one hundred thousand supporters from all states in the Republic of Mexico for the March of the Color of the Earth on March 11, 2001, in Mexico City. They demanded that the government stop the mistreatment of the poor, illiterate, and disenfranchised Indigenous people who made up approximately 10 percent of their population of one hundred million.[1] They were called rebels, just like our suffering servant, Jesus, whose life and earthly ministry and advocacy have informed us that the right way is not always the most popular way. Meekness does not equal weakness; it does not equal indifference or idleness. Meekness is the spiritual way of Jesus. It must be exercised in humility and in public, for it can bring earthly powers to their knees. The meek will surely inherit the earth.

TWENTY-THREE

A Heart That Speaks Wisdom and Justice

The mouths of the righteous utter wisdom,
   and their tongues speak what is just.
The law of their God is in their hearts;
   their feet do not slip.

Psalm 37:30–31

Ka Richards is the wife of African American pastor Jahill, the mother of five, and a grandmother. As a Hmong American daughter of refugees, she grew up in impoverished multiethnic communities. She currently ministers in a predominately African American context, is a Charles Simeon Trust instructor, and is a contributor to the book *His Testimonies, My Heritage: Women of Color on the Word of God.*

God's Word teaches us that a believer's speech should be marked by wisdom and justice. These two marks are the result of having God's instruction rooted in our hearts (Ps. 37:31). Jesus knows that the tongue speaks what overflows out of the abundance of one's heart (Luke 6:45). In other words, when our hearts are filled with God's Word, we will do what is right (Ps. 37:31), utter wisdom, and speak what is just (v. 30).

The Mouths of the Wise and the Just

The mouth that utters wisdom (Ps. 37:30) can speak wisely into a world full of evil, betrayal, and brokenness. In these verses, I'm reminded of the older, godly, and wise women who surround me. Women like my spiritual mother, Kristie, who "opens her mouth with wisdom" and has kindness "on her tongue" (Prov. 31:26 ESV); and my natural mother, Song, who wisely counseled my father to flee the country of Laos so our family could take refuge in Thailand during the Hmong genocide.

The one who speaks what is just (Ps. 37:30) not only speaks of what is right but also speaks against what is wrong. As believers, we must "speak up for those who have no voice, for the justice of all who are dispossessed" (Prov. 31:8 CSB). The Lord loves justice (Ps. 37:28) and requires his children to "do justice, and to love kindness, and to walk humbly" with him (Mic. 6:8 ESV). There are various ways "doing justice" can be expressed.

In some cases, wisdom and justice are carried out by telling the stories of oppressed people like my own, the Hmong people. We have faced ethnic and political oppression for over two hundred years and continue to fight for our dignity and liberty. Many of our people are exiles from our original homeland—a people dispossessed, who were forced to flee from south China to Laos, and from Laos to refugee camps in Thailand, then to numerous places around the globe. Wisdom and justice cry out for our stories to be told.

Speaking Wisdom and Justice from Our Past Sorrows

Most Americans have never heard of the Hmong people who contributed greatly to American history. During the Vietnam War, there was a covert US operation—a "secret war" in Laos—led by the CIA.[1] It was a US war fought against Lao and Vietnamese communists, not with soldiers from the United States but with tens of thousands of hired Hmong tribesmen. The United States promised my people that if we helped them fight, they would take care of us, "win or lose."[2]

The US knew that the war was a lost cause but continued to deploy Hmong soldiers into battle.[3] My father, Boua, fought in the war for six years until he was shot and severely injured during combat. In God's mercy, he survived, but many who fought side by side with him did not return home. Generations of our men were slaughtered. So many Hmong soldiers were dying in the war that young boys, some as young as ten years old, were recruited and trained for only three days before going into battle. After inadequate training, they were sent out as special guerilla units to fight on the front lines of the secret war against well-trained and seasoned Lao/Vietnamese communist militants.[4] Forcing ten-year-old boys to become child soldiers and fight a civil war is inhumane!

In 1973, President Nixon signed the Paris Peace Accord, and the US military pulled out of Laos and Vietnam—deserting the Hmong people and leaving them to fend for themselves. As a result, the Lao communists started a Hmong genocide. Between 1975 and 1985, more than 150,000 Hmong people lost their lives trying to flee from Laos.[5] The Hmong genocide continues to this day, and my people are still being hunted down like animals, raped, tortured, and slaughtered in the jungles of Laos. Because of this, they are always on the run.

One woman shares that while she was giving birth, the Lao communists attacked. She had to pick up her baby and run, with no time to cut her umbilical cord.[6]

My people are still waiting and hopeful that the Americans will keep their promise and return to help them because of their sacrifices during the war.[7] Where is help for my people who are being annihilated today? When all feels hopeless, God's Word tells us not to put our trust in humans, who cannot save, but to call upon the name of the Lord Jesus. He is near to the brokenhearted and saves the crushed in spirit (Ps. 34:18; Ps. 146:3; Rom. 10:13). He will write his Word in our hearts so we will not slip into despair (Ps. 37:31).

Our stories and place in American history have been mostly concealed. This injustice dishonors Hmong people, including the honorable men, women, and children who died during the secret war. It reveals America's folly in hiding their complicity in the war and the Hmong genocide by not coming to the aid of their allies. In an effort to cover up and save face, America is also guilty of suppressing the stories and voices of ethnic people groups on the margins.

Unlike those who do not have the law of God in their hearts, as representatives of Jesus and his kingdom, we do. So we must speak up! We must speak wisdom and justice (Ps. 37:30–31) into unjust systems and circumstances that turn a blind eye to the oppressed.

Speaking Wisdom and Seeking Justice amid Contemporary Sorrows

In modern times, Asian communities have fallen victim to increased racist attacks as a result of an American president whose mouth consistently uttered folly, giving full vent to his rage (Prov. 29:11; Isa. 32:6). I saw a video of an elderly Hmong woman getting kicked in the face while waiting for a bus transit.[8] I heard of a man stabbing an Asian American family (including a two-year-old and six-year-old) for fear of them spreading COVID-19,[9] and another story of an eighty-nine-year-old Asian grandmother being set on fire.[10] It's utterly disgusting, and I've wept many times hearing about these brutalities.

In the Lord's mercy, he has sent many Black brothers and sisters in the Lord to stand in solidarity with Asians at this critical time.[11] They have been a beautiful example of what it looks like to "love your neighbor as yourself" (Mark 12:31). Black people in America know and understand this struggle and fight for justice. They have been doing it for a long time, so it is not hard for them to respond when they see the same racial injustices happening to other people[12]— like in 2006, when Fong, a nineteen-year-old Hmong man, was the victim of police brutality and died. His mother said that the first people to show up in support of her family were from the Black community.[13] Consequently, this mother actively participated in protests after George Floyd was murdered by police.[14]

Similarly, because our Black brothers and sisters are speaking against anti-Asian attacks, I've witnessed many Asians speak up and stand in solidarity with the Black community against racism, police brutality, and other injustices, unlike before, when many Asians were silent.[15] Black and Asian solidarity is beautiful and is no small thing. It may even be a historical turning point in the history of conflict and tension between Blacks and Asians.[16]

As a Hmong American married to a Black husband, and parent of Black and Asian children, this solidarity causes my heart to greatly rejoice! When I look at my children, I'm reminded of the long legacies that Hmong and Black people have in fighting for freedom. I tell them that justice runs in their veins. The secret "civil" war was going on around the same time as the United States Civil Rights Movement, so their history and bloodline embody perseverance through many afflictions, slavery, and genocides. I tell them that as justified people, we are called to live just lives and to use our tongues to speak what is just, uttering wisdom with the law of God in our hearts. We won't slip into silence or complicity if we obey God's Word. Rather, we will walk in the footsteps of Jesus (Ps. 37:30–31; 1 John 2:6).

To the Suffering Servant and Victorious King, we lift up our voices. You know our pain and suffering all too well. We cry out to you for justice, and we ask that you exalt the lowly and bring the oppressed into your green pastures. We ask that you extend mercy and salvation to the oppressors who've used their power to enslave and murder people who are fearfully and wonderfully made in your image. In Jesus's name. Amen.

Marny Xiong (1989–2020)

A Fighter for Justice

When she saw injustices against her peers and communities,
she made it her issue to fight back to hold people
and institutions accountable.[17]

Marny Xiong was a Hmong American daughter of refugees who barely escaped the Hmong genocide in Laos. Friends and family remember her as an activist for racial justice and education equality. She had a keen awareness of structural inequality and saw that many of America's policies were not created to support communities of color.[18]

In 2006, as a student at the University of Minnesota Duluth, she organized a campaign consisting of Black, Asian, and Hispanic students to convince administrators to conduct one of its first campus climate surveys and to start a Black Studies degree program. She would later go on to become the first Hmong woman that I am aware of to get a minor in Black Studies.[19]

In 2008, when the Minneapolis Police Department awarded Officer Jason Anderson the medal of valor after he shot nineteen-year-old Fong Lee three times in the back and then five times on the ground during a foot chase, falsely claiming that Fong had a gun and attempted to aim it at him,[20] Marny helped put on a series of rallies until the department rescinded the award.[21] She was not the type of person to overlook structural injustice, no matter the institution.

Minnesota has one of the largest education disparities in the nation between whites and people of color.[22] Because of her passion to see change in the school systems and equity for all students, Marny ran for the Saint Paul school board in 2017 and was successful.

While on the school board, she worked on mending the relationships between Black, Asian, and Hispanic communities and the district's majority-white teaching staff, administration, and school board.[23] Later, she became the board chair.

After President Trump started using the term "Chinese virus" and anti-Asian hate crimes spiked,[24] Marny started a campaign for Minnesota's Asian American elected officials to write a letter denouncing racism.[25]

Amid Marny's fight for justice and equality for the marginalized, she fell ill to the coronavirus. After about a month of fighting for her life, she died on June 7, 2020. She was thirty-one years old.[26] In life and death, Marny was a fighter, and she will be remembered because of her fight for justice.[27] This image bearer spoke wisdom and justice into specific areas of need and, in so doing, reflected God's heart. She used her voice to "speak up" for the oppressed (Prov. 31:8–9). Will you?

TWENTY-FOUR

Owning My Heritage as Queen

> Wicked people watch good people
>   and try to kill them;
> but the LORD will not abandon them to their
>   enemy's power
>   or let them be condemned when they are on trial.
>
> Psalm 37:32–33 GNT

Rebecca Deng is the author of *What They Meant for Evil: How a Lost Girl of Sudan Found Healing, Peace, and Purpose in the Midst of Suffering* and is one of the eighty-nine Lost Girls of Sudan who came to the US in 2000. She is an international speaker and advocate for those victimized by war. She is African American of South Sudanese origin.

What if women owned their narratives and how we all speak of them?

The ancient land of Nubia and Kush—known today as Sudan, South Sudan, and Ethiopia—is a land of royal women. These women were queens, warriors, and leaders of their people, and they had influence over the international diplomacy of their time. While the stories of most have been lost, we do know about "the Candaces of Meroe" and the queens—like the one

Luke mentions in Acts 8:27—who ruled the Kingdom of Kush from the city of Meroe between c. 284 BCE and 314 CE.[1] Since c. 284 BCE, royal women bore the honorable titles of Queen Mother and Queen Regent, identifying either the mother of the king or a female monarch who ruled alongside a king.[2] This long-standing tradition saw men and women as equals.

Additionally, Queen Candace Shanakdakhete (70 BCE) and several women after her ruled independently.[3] The leadership of these courageous and strong women led to established trade routes and the flourishing of their communities and paved the way for leaders of the modern world like Commander Ager Gum. Commander Gum gained respect for her role in the Sudanese Civil War (1983–2005), and she rose as a heroine of the South Sudanese Liberation Struggle.[4] These stories reveal the true power of African women and their leadership, and I am honored to know and carry them with me.

The Women Who Raised Me

While ancient tribal women had the luxury of deep peace in a place they knew and were known, the present diaspora of Black African women continue to struggle. Growing up in the late 1990s and early 2000s, I didn't see my father much because he was a commander in the Sudan People's Liberation Army/Movement. Most of my friends didn't have their fathers around either, but we had a lot of women raising us. These women led in villages, towns, churches, internally displaced people camps, and refugee camps in neighboring countries. Unlike the wicked who "lie in wait for the righteous" (Ps. 37:32), these women were peacemakers between groups in conflict. They served sick and orphaned children the food rations received from the United Nations. They were our mentors before we arrived in the United States as the "Lost Boys and Lost Girls of Sudan."

Today, the majority of Sudanese women in the US work low-paying jobs, but they send remittances to relatives living in war-torn countries and refugee camps while still taking care of their US communities. They feed families who have lost loved ones, gotten sick, or had a baby. Whenever possible, they will not allow the most vulnerable to see a premature death. Like our royal ancestors, they are robed in honor. At Sudanese celebrations, you will notice their nobility through the wearing of their perfume, their style of dress, their decorative painted henna, and their gold jewelry. Some of the women arrive to the gathering straight from night-shift work, but you can't detect any distress in their faces. God has not left them in the powerful hands of the wicked, so they walk with grace, resilience, and beauty as they dance, serve food, or exchange jokes and laughter. Because "she is clothed with strength and dignity; she can laugh at the days to come" (Prov. 31:25).

While we struggle to maintain our dignity, royal heritage, and respect, there is an unspoken grief among us. Some of us have lost ourselves and have lost our way. We have been uprooted from our traditions, languages, and ways of life, and we haven't found solid footing to function as Black women in America. The fading culture is apparent. When the women sing traditional songs, some of them struggle to sing along or dance authentically to the beat of the drum. This is a tension we knew nothing about before our arrival.

The Wicked Lie in Wait

The wicked want us to hate and kill ourselves. As Black women, we are pressured to perform under social constructs that are sometimes not clear *to* or meant *for* us, and so we are constantly rejected. We worry about our skin color, the texture of our hair, and other societal expectations. We hold up pillars of everyday life, which leaves us with no time to reflect and be creative. We are constantly giving.

The wicked want us to hate and kill our bodies. Some Sudanese women have accepted the distorted narrative of being "fair" and "lovely," and have therefore rejected their God-given complexion which has stolen the hearts of men from the beginning of time. Even Moses fell for a Black beauty, a woman from the land of Kush, and his family was against it (Num. 12:1). Some of us believe that our skin is an obstacle to "fitting in" or getting jobs. Additionally, we know the standards of beauty in Western culture, so some Sudanese women use skin-lightening products to feel beautiful and to gain a sense of belonging in their new land. These creams are dangerous for our health and are quite costly.[5]

> *Creator, God of our complexion and the one whose image we bear, may we be content with whatever color you created us to be and wear it with pride and nobility like our ancestors did. May the wicked in companies that make money selling and advertising harmful chemical creams be held accountable.*

I'm Not the One on Trial

When I arrived in the United States at fifteen years old with zero education or knowledge of how to function in this new land, it would have been helpful to have mentors of color to guide my navigation of this new reality. As I grew into adulthood, initial encounters with injustice in the US informed my understanding that this society views me as a headache instead of an asset or balm to bring about change and healing. I didn't know what to do with this new experience that remains in contrast to my formative years. In South Sudan, I grew up with Black privilege, where I didn't have to think about my skin color or what it meant to be "Black," but at some point, that sense of being and belonging changed when I arrived in the United States.

Even today, every time I step out in the US with my dark skin, I am reminded that I am different simply because of the questions that some people ask. When playing with my kids, who are a lighter complexion, I have been asked if I am their babysitter. At other times, I've been questioned if the address on my driver's license is the correct one, assuming I do not belong in a designated neighborhood.

These experiences were initially confusing to me as an adult because when I was growing up in my white foster family's home, they commonly said to me, "The world is your oyster." When I entered the real world as a grown Black woman, however, the world became a trap instead of a beautifully open place to live free, to explore, and to co-labor in the work God calls each of us to do. Like so many Black women, my true voice began to coil up, and I put it away to adopt new voices to survive, but it didn't take long for my body to reject those foreign voices. Yes, I want to keep a job and food on the table, and I also want to live.

The Lord Protects the Innocent

Africa's modern-day wars and famine target Black women and their children. Rape is commonly used as a weapon of war, and as a result, a United Nations official nicknamed the Democratic Republic of Congo the "rape capital" of the world.[6] Today, there are girls and boys on the streets—of what was once the ancient civilization of Kush—now living without families to care for them. The effects of war and high levels of poverty leave young people without hope, safety, or a structured life. The jails are full of women, girls, and boys whose parents and ancestors used to run free in their gardens, raise cattle, and grow sorghum along the Nile. The uprooting and colonization of tribes have come with new habits such as drinking, drug usage, and increased violence. These crimes were not common before the

Sudanese people's culture and norms were destroyed by war. There are no institutions or local organizations that are equipped to deal with these new realities, so the Sudanese women are wailing, mourning their lost roots and deep connections to their land and their way of life.

The violence of war has caused forced and voluntary immigration and has led me to a foreign land. While the wicked have brought all kinds of injustices against the most vulnerable and righteous of my people, God has not abandoned us. He has brought down powerful thrones before, and the righteous Judge is able to do it again in this life or the next.

God of transformation and Redeemer of all things, restore us back to our true selves to seek you and bring justice to the world. Amen.

Adol Bior (1830–80)

My Maternal Great-Great-Great-Great-Great-Grandmother

Don't Let Adol Bior Turn in Her Grave

Adol Bior was born and raised in South Sudan, which was once known as Kush. In her Jieng and Dinka traditions, owning a home was associated with women. Jieng men don't own a house until they are married; they might be old enough and financially stable, but if they are not married, they live under a relative's roof. In Adol's time, women were the community leaders, and baby boys and girls were treated as equals.

Adol was married to Kuot Anuet, and she was the matriarch of our family. It became the tradition for some of the Jieng Adol clan to name their firstborn daughters Adol in honor of the matriarch. This tradition is still practiced today. Several songs and sayings about Adol Bior indicate that she was an alpha female among her people.

While she was recognized and supported as matriarch by her tribe, Adol knew her own truth, value, and calling. She knew how to read her people's hearts and advocate for their well-being. Gifted in hospitality and strategic leadership, she gathered wisdom from her Creator, the giver of life. Many of her kinship, foreigners, and strangers passed through her land and stopped at her simple hut house to receive the blessing of her warm food. She believed that hunger was the fastest way to destroy humans, and so she made it her calling to provide food for those whose feet graced her house.

Much like the prophetess Deborah, who served as a judge in the Bible (Judg. 4), Adol used her home to settle affairs for the rest of her family and disagreements within the community. Even today, the belief remains that if your mother came from Adol's clan, you are likely to become a leader. Adol was a true queen, advocate, and worker of goodness for her people. In an equitable world, the story of Adol Bior and many Black women leaders of South Sudan like her would be recorded in history books alongside the Western feminists and matriarchs we learn about in school, but her history was stolen and ignored. I lift up her name now so she will never be forgotten.

If Adol were still here, I think she might ask of modern South Sudanese, "Where are your women? Why aren't today's women in leadership positions like the tribal women of the past? Why are you doing worse in the twenty-first century, when the words *equality*, *feminism*, and *inclusion* are on the lips of so many? Where are you culturally, spiritually, and geographically?" Even now, she beckons me to take my place as a "Queen Regent." As a queen, I say, "Old women, rise up! Young girls, you also rise! And yes, we need our brothers to become co-laborers to join hands with us as we claim the lost traditions of kingdom partnership and honor women's leadership for the good of the people." We have led before, and we can certainly do it again.

STROPHE 7

PSALM 37:34–40

TWENTY-FIVE

Release in Me a Song of Lament

A Poem by Grace P. Cho, Korean American Writer

My grandma used to wrap her thumb
Tight with a thread
Gathering the blood at the top
With thumb bent over
She'd take a needle and prick the skin
Right beneath her nail
To ease the unmoving pain stuck
Between her gut and chest
Dark blood would trickle out
And she'd wipe it away
Red drops smeared on white

With each squeeze
The knots would untangle
Releasing the tension within
Each prick pushed the dark blood out
Until it turned brighter
A sign that she'd done what was needed
Unthreading her thumb
The color would return
Life flowing freely again

When I was young and my stomach
Would be tied up in knots

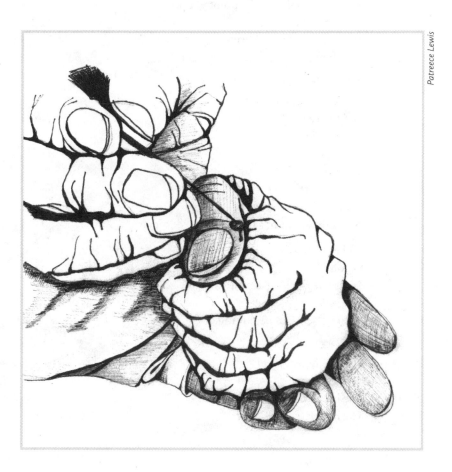

My grandma would try to prick my thumb
To help me
In love
But I could only see the pointed tip
Of the needle
And too afraid of the prick
I was willing to hold on to my pain

White in the face
I'd protest her efforts
And turn away from
The relief promised
She'd give up because
It was no use forcing someone
To receive the help
They so desperately needed
When they couldn't see their own desperation

And now
Rage and grief
Twist like thick rope inside me
Tangled
With no sense of beginning or end

Tears are caged by
The numbness I feel
The violence
The helplessness
The hopelessness I feel

Cursing overtakes
My language
But I can't seem
To put to sound
The screams stuck
Within me

Someone help me!
  Release this overwhelming pain
  Before it overcomes me
Someone show me!
  How to guide this anger
  Before it hardens my empathy
  My vision for what could be

I want to resist hope
Until the wicked perish
Until justice is given

But if I'm honest—
I'm desperate
For a reason to keep going
Toward a future that looks
Nothing like it is now

I'm searching
For a way forward
So I look back
To my history
And remember

My people who held on
Through oppression
And forced assimilation
The women of my heritage
Who beat their chests
Pounding out their lament
Through minor notes
Of song and prayer

I call out—
I'm ready, Halmoni!
Come prick my heart

But if I'm honest—
I'm desperate
For a reason to keep going
Toward a future that looks
Nothing like it is now

Wrap me with your thread of resilience
I'm bent low
No longer afraid of the needle
More afraid of becoming like stone
Come prick me
And make me tender again
Let the cynicism flow out of me

Show me
How to wail and whimper
Weep and scream
The anguish
Through guttural cries
Teach me the rhythm
Of pounding my chest
And loosen my lips
To sing the notes of lament

She takes the needle
And pricks my soul
The anger and grief
Flow mingled down
She wipes my tears
Smoothes my hair
And says,
Shhh, one day
One day
There will be peace

We sing in harmony
Our song of lament
And the sounds become words
Of hopeful praise

Hallelujah
A day will come
A day will come
Hallelujah

Grace P. Cho is a Korean American writer, poet, and speaker, and the editorial manager at (in)courage. She creates space for people to be known, nurtured, and challenged through her work and desires to elevate Women of Color's voices in the publishing industry.

TWENTY-SIX

Why Women Wail

A Litany by Patricia Raybon, African American Author

Hope in the LORD
    and keep his way.
He will exalt you to inherit the land;
    when the wicked are destroyed, you will see it.

Psalm 37:34

From the editor: An early editor of Psalm 37 sought to improve the acrostic poem by adding verse 34 after noticing that the Hebrew letter qoph (ק) was missing. Diverging from the author's original intent, this verse serves as an exhortation. The call-and-response practice from the African American church invites us into the liturgical purposes of this addition to the psalm. The spiritual practice of corporate worship and this verse connect Black suffering to Black joy, Black hope to Black liberation. By sharing this practice steeped in history and tradition, we invite other people groups to connect with God, trust and hope in him, and obediently follow in his way.

From the author: This liturgy invites gatherings of faith to honor the leader's call declaring why women wail by responding with an affirmation. The response establishes a unifying spirit within the congregation, rendering a spiritual harmony amid worshipers, letting the leader know that she is speaking good truth to their souls, bathing their hearts with the honesty that change requires. So, here's some feedback, leader, to encourage you to continue. Heard stylistically in Black preaching, praising, and singing—and also in African American musical contexts such as jazz and the blues—the call-and-response presented here is in an honoring format designed to acknowledge the tradition of the format and the significance of the call declaring why Women of Color wail. Blessings as you take part in this truth-telling litany.

LEADER: *Of course.* We wail for all the doggone wrong done to us, and done to all the women and girls and babies who look like us, and all the ways that wrong was waged against us, even in the blessed name of holy Jesus.

PEOPLE: His faithful love endures forever.

LEADER: We wail for being told to get back, shut yo' mouth, wait over there, stand yourself down, and hold your tongue while others talked over us, about us, at us, and against us as if we weren't even in the room.

PEOPLE: His faithful love endures forever.

LEADER: We wail for being called gal and "nigra" and Sal and Mammy and "you people" and "whatever"—and not one of those things is even our name and, to tell the truth, it never was.

PEOPLE: His faithful love endures forever.

LEADER: We wail for cages that hold children and Mylar blankets that hold tears.

PEOPLE: His faithful love endures forever.

LEADER: We wail for Sojourner Truth, who bore five children, one dead too soon, the other four sold out from under her without a shred of concern for their pain and sorrow, not to mention hers—or the pain of the millions of unknown women who endured the same godawful thing.

PEOPLE: His faithful love endures forever.

LEADER: We wail for the Iroquois and the Mohawk and the Pequot and the Oneida and the Seneca and the Arapaho and the Navajo and the Cherokee and the Ute and the other Native populations in North America reduced by nine million to a remnant now of barely three million by broken promises and treaties and will and sheer hate.

PEOPLE: His faithful love endures forever.

LEADER: We wail for being told not to be so angry all the time, even when we were just asking a question about what happened or when we spoke out about a wrong.

PEOPLE: His faithful love endures forever.

LEADER: We wail for the Chinese Exclusion Act, Executive Order 9066, and anti-Asian hate—for Manzanar and Amache and Topaz and Heart Mountain and every other internment camp and edict and rule devised to shackle the lives and kill the spirits of defenseless people because they weren't white.

PEOPLE: His faithful love endures forever.

LEADER: We wail for the Muslim ban and hate crimes at mosques and Islamophobic lies based on fears and ugly myths and supremacists' views that look down on others.

PEOPLE: His faithful love endures forever.

LEADER: We wail for being told we don't want to be successful, even after standing at the bus stop at 5:00 a.m. to get to the first of our three jobs in one day to put food on our tables and clothes on the backs of our children who got suspended from school for acting their age in class.

PEOPLE: His faithful love endures forever.

LEADER: We wail for a novel coronavirus called COVID-19 and vaccine distribution so disproportionate—and conspiracy theories so alarming—that, globally, people have died in horrifying numbers.

PEOPLE: His faithful love endures forever.

LEADER: We wail for those who deny voting rights, won't support universal health care, the human rights of immigrants, or environmental justice, even if the policies give and spare lives.

PEOPLE: His faithful love endures forever.

LEADER: We wail for Emmett Till and the four little Birmingham girls (Addie Mae Collins, Cynthia Wesley, Carole Robertson, and Carol Denise McNair), for Medgar Evers and Trayvon Martin, for Breonna Taylor and Anjanette Young, for Rayshard Brooks and Atatiana Jefferson, for Stephon Clark and Sandra Bland, for Botham

Jean and Dajerria Becton, for George Floyd and Ahmaud Arbery, for Ma'Khia Bryant, and too many others whose names were never widely said or known or acknowledged or cried over.

PEOPLE: His faithful love endures forever.

LEADER: We wail for being called victimizers when we speak up about all that has victimized us.

PEOPLE: His faithful love endures forever.

LEADER: We wail for having to laugh when nothing was funny, cry when nobody cared, explain when the obvious was clear.

PEOPLE: His faithful love endures forever.

LEADER: We wail to a God who promises to see us, hear us, walk with us, and go before us.

PEOPLE: His faithful love endures forever.

LEADER: We wail. Knowing God listens. Even if others won't. His faithful love endures forever. Thus, in him, we wail so nobody can ever say we didn't trust God to turn it around.

Patricia Raybon is an award-winning Colorado author, essayist, and novelist who writes stories of faith and mystery. Her debut 1920s mystery novel, *All That Is Secret: An Annalee Spain Mystery*, was a *Parade* magazine fall 2021 "Mysteries We Love" selection and a PBS *Masterpiece*'s "Best Mystery Books of 2021: As Recommended by Bestselling Authors." As an African American follower of Christ, she encourages people globally to love God and each other.

TWENTY-SEVEN

The Tree That Withers

I have seen a wicked and ruthless man
    flourishing like a luxuriant native tree,
but he soon passed away and was no more;
    though I looked for him, he could not be found.

Psalm 37:35–36

Dennae Pierre is co-director for The Crete Collective, City to
City North America, and director of The Surge Network. She
serves at Roosevelt Community Church, a multiethnic church in
downtown Phoenix. Dennae is Latina and grew up in a mixed-
culture home that introduced her to the importance of bridging
cultures.

Phoenix is a city that has been known across our nation for
hostility toward immigrants and harsh anti-immigration
policies. For twenty-four years, we had Sheriff Joe Arpaio, who
dubbed himself "America's Toughest Sheriff."[1] In 2010, he led
the charge in Arizona's passing of legislation SB 1070,[2] which
became known as one of the nation's harshest anti-immigration
legislations. During this season, thousands of homes were raided
without warrants; churches in Spanish-speaking, low-income
communities were harassed by the sheriff's deputies; and mass
deportation resulted in thousands of families separated. The

legislation was eventually struck down by the US Supreme Court, and Sheriff Joe was charged with contempt of court for violating court orders and continuing racial profiling.[3] Within Arizona, it seemed Sheriff Joe was beloved and celebrated by the masses, yet for many immigrant families, he symbolized hate and invoked a great amount of fear. For decades, he seemed to flourish without consequence.

Trees That Wither

The "wicked and ruthless man" that the psalmist describes in Psalm 37:35–36 is not simply an unrighteous individual but a person who has power.[4] The ruthlessness of the powerful can invoke terror in those who are on the receiving end of their wickedness. At a simple glance, the wicked seem to prosper and succeed in their plans and there seems to be no end in sight to the fear they invoke, but the psalmist provides a powerful metaphor to remind the reader of the finite power and fragile life of the wicked.

> The wicked are like a beautiful native tree.
> Gaze and wonder, if you'd like. How did it establish itself?
> If you want, consider how it prospers?
> But don't spend too long, for in the blink of an eye,
> it will disappear and leave no trace of its existence.
> (Ps. 37:35–36, paraphrase)

The wicked are compared to a luxuriant native tree that soon passes away and is no more. This is a significant contrast to the tree in Psalm 1, a simile that the psalmist uses to describe the righteous, whose "delight is in the law of the LORD and [who] meditates on it day and night. [This] person is like a tree planted by streams of water, which yields its fruit in season and whose leaf does not wither"

(Ps. 1:2–3). On the contrary, the tree that describes the wicked does not have deep roots. There is no source to draw on day and night; therefore, that tree is fleeting. As quickly as it sprung up, it will be chopped down or will wither away (Ps. 37:36). It can be tempting to despair as the wicked seem to prosper year after year, especially for the one who suffers from their tactics, but the psalmist wants the reader to understand that no matter what prosperity of the wicked looks like at first glance, the shallow roots beneath ensure the ways of the wicked cannot last.

Trees Planted by Streams of Water

The harsh immigration policies and divisive rhetoric that surrounded SB 1070 resulted in countless immigrant families being afraid to leave their homes. Children would describe feeling sick at school because they were witnessing mass deportation, and they did not know if their parents would be home when they returned. Hundreds of people were held in immigration detention centers for years without court dates. Amid all the challenges, a generation of Latinos emerged as leaders, advocates, and organizers for change. As young people organized to resist immigration legislation, they were hopeful that the hostility and consistent assault on immigrant families would not endure forever.

Eventually, through nonviolent protesting and community organizing, the legislation was kept in the public eye as the immigrant community waited for the Supreme Court to overturn it. Nearly six years of organized protests, activism, and nonviolent campaigns along with a lawsuit filed by many immigrant rights organizations resulted in nullifying SB 1070.[5] When victims of injustice or violence coalesce their power and share a collective voice, the world is reminded just how frail power is for the wicked and ruthless.

The wicked are not merely adversaries to God's people; their actions are acts of defiance against God himself. Resisting God's ways will result in substantial consequences. Years, decades, or even generations may pass, but there will come a moment when the fruit of their actions will erode their influence and power. As Psalm 73 reminds us, they will ultimately face God in this life and in the life eternal. Despite even temporary flourishing, the "slippery ground" (v. 18) of evil will lead them to destruction and terror. They will awaken, only to discover that the life they chose was but a fantasy in God's eyes (v. 20). They will perish. God will wipe away all remnants of unfaithfulness, and only those who take refuge in God will remain.

In the face of the ruthlessness of the wicked, God's people can sometimes hide, despair, minimize, or even mimic the same evil patterns to survive or get ahead. The withering tree is a symbol intended to warn and instruct God's people. They are not to envy the ruthless man or yield to their bitterness. There is no place for resignation or surrender. Rather, the righteous are to live firmly planted—like the tree in Psalm 1—in God's reality. They are empowered by God's Spirit or living water to resist the schemes of the evil one. God's people should be the first to point out the shallow roots beneath the surface of what seems to prosper and the first to assemble a faithful, hope-filled, and persevering response. The leaves of this tree will not wither, and this tree will surely yield fruit in due season (Ps. 1:3).

Father, we are exasperated and weary as we go year after year watching the wicked flourish. They seem to prosper even while striking terror and harming the vulnerable. We witness generations wondering whether the wicked will pay any consequence for profaning your name, and we watch as the ruthless succeed in misusing power. Yet, we know that every act of injustice, every attempt to prosper at the expense of our neighbors is an assault on the very way you designed and ordered your world. Lord, may the ways of wickedness be confronted by your holy and righteous love, starting with us. Expose and reveal any part of our lives that does not align with your righteousness. Empower us to resist ruthlessness, and establish us in your ways of love, truth, and peace. Amen.

Eva Carrillo de García (1883–1979)

La Vanguardia[6]

Eva Carrillo de García is an example of a woman who flourished while pursuing a righteous life of advocacy, deep concern for the vulnerable, and a resistance to wickedness. She was a missionary, nurse, social welfare volunteer, civil rights activist, wife, and mother of eight children. She was born in Los Angeles, California, where her mother died from typhoid fever before Eva was five years old. Her father remarried, and she eventually became a ward of the Methodist Church, assigned to the local missionary Dr. Levi Salmans. Dr. Salmans was the first Methodist medical missionary in Mexico, and he took Eva with him to work and study there.

Eva attended college in Guanajuato, Mexico, and later she moved to Kansas to attend Bethany Hospital, a school for nursing, where she graduated in 1906. She went on to graduate from the Chicago Training School for City, Home, and Foreign Missions, and she became a nurse at Battle Creek Sanitarium in Battle Creek, Michigan. There, she met her husband, Dr. Alberto G. García. Eva and her husband worked in an orphanage in San Juan, Puerto Rico, as well as in Mexico and Central America, until they returned to settle down in Austin, Texas.

In Austin, Eva and her husband published *La Vanguardia*, the first Spanish-language newspaper published in Austin.[7] As a nurse and advocate of public health, she also worked diligently to organize mass distribution of information to prevent tuberculosis. They used the newspaper to encourage Austin's Latino community to buy property, engage in politics, vote, and work together to advocate for their rights.

Eva was born into an ethnically segregated world as well as one in which women did not have the right to vote. She joined the League of Women Voters of Texas, where she became an active member and went on to become one of the founding members and president of the Ladies League of United Latin American Citizens (LULAC) in Austin. Through these platforms, she advocated for women's right to vote and worked to desegregate movie theaters, swimming pools, and schools.

In addition to her tireless work for justice, public health, and empowering and organizing Latinos, Eva also provided leadership to the local church. She was an elder at University Methodist Church and helped start the second Mexican American church in Austin— Emmanuel Methodist. Through her church, she collaborated with city probation officers and juvenile agencies to engage young people and help turn them from delinquency. The life of Eva Carrillo de García is a powerful story that reveals a woman with significant leadership capacity, countless passions, holistic engagement in society, and perseverance to resist structures that needed dismantling so that all could flourish.[8]

TWENTY-EIGHT

Live in a Good Way

Notice good people, observe the righteous;
peaceful people have descendants,
but sinners are completely destroyed,
and their descendants are wiped out.

Psalm 37:37–38 GNT

Renee Kylestewa Begay is from the Pueblo of Zuni, located in the southwestern part of New Mexico. She is married to her high school sweetheart, Donnie Begay, and they have three daughters. She is the national director for Nations, a conference speaker, and manages a resource website called The Talking Circle. She founded the Nations movement—a national ministry that seeks to build relationships with the Native American community.

What does it mean to live as a "good" person? The word itself can stir up conflicting definitions. I come from an Indigenous identity, and my identity itself has had standards set on it to prove its goodness and righteousness. At different stages of my faith in Jesus, I have been painfully reminded of the standards that define my goodness. I've been told that I must throw off my Indigenous practices because those practices are sinful to God. I've been told that I must concentrate only on Jesus because any cultural addition or any expression of my

Indigenous rituals are sinful distractions. When it comes to living and becoming a good person, I have learned to ask myself, "Where lies the myth?"

Psalm 37:37–38 challenges me to take note and observe the good person. The verses imply that perhaps there are good people from every community, every household, every village. For we all live by a set of formulated values. *How do these values play themselves out to ensure descendants? Where have I seen values of certain people and imaginations bring destruction?* I am thankful for the simplicity of the Scripture. It does not specify that goodness comes only from a certain individual, a certain region, or a certain worldview. Every community contains stories of goodness. Find them. Observe them.

The Scripture calls me to see the collective Indigenous identity as good even when we've been told otherwise. I have a right to see the goodness in myself because I bear the image of the Creator's goodness. I have a freedom to celebrate the goodness of my people's existence and the valuable practices of goodness they've taught me. If we consider the promise of verses 37–38, wouldn't the Indigenous peoples of this continent be considered good since our ways of knowing and being are very much alive after all these centuries? For it is my people who have taught me the good ways of our Creator. I have been taught to commit to these values:

- Hon delanko'ha:willi:wa—"We will be empathetic with one another."

  In living as a community, we remember our moments of pain and grief during life's complexities. In remembrance of these moments, we can consider the experiences of others and give full weight and validity to their feelings. We can offer patience, shared grief, and an encouraging word.

- Hon i:yayyułashik'yana:wa—"We will respect one another."

  In living as a community, we respect one another's physical and spiritual boundaries as well as boundaries of location. We discourage the need to overtake one another in body, in belief, and in our land.

- Hon ko'hoł lewuna:wediyahnan, wan hon i:tse'manna—"We will think before we act and consider how the consequences of our actions will affect others."

  There is a ripple effect to our actions; therefore, we must be mindful about what our hearts want to accomplish. We are asked to consider how our actions, our words, and our behaviors will affect others around us. In preparing our actions, we must seek permission from the appropriate people of authority, and we must act in a way that serves the health and wholeness of ourselves and our community.

Take notice: This is what it means to live an upright and peaceful life. This is the way that we can teach our children and their children, so we do not continually destroy each other or wipe out communities of people who are made in the image of the Creator.

Our good Creator, you have formed Indigenous people with their own origin stories. We reflect the goodness of your Being. You looked at us and said, "You are good." We have been present since time immemorial, yet we are forgotten and overlooked.

Instead of honoring our heritage and our dignity, a dominating society has categorized our values and profanely called our sacred ways syncretistic, savage, irredeemable, and somehow evil. Will you let these abusive stereotypes continue? They have used their perceptions to justify wiping out our existence and taking our land. How will you help them see that we, too, are living with your Spirit within us? When will the Christian body realize that it needs us? When will they come to see us as human beings who are made in your image? Creator God, what do you see when you see my people? Do you see the same as they do?

When will you help us? When will you tell them that you know us? How do we know if we are good when others continually tell us that we are sinners? While our prayers teach us to live in harmonious balance, how long will it take for others to see us, to recognize us, to come visit us, to listen and learn about how we have lived in a good way for thousands of years? Whom do we call out to when we desire to exist for the blessing of our descendants? If not you, then to whom do we turn, oh Lord, our Creator?

The Zuni People: Ulohnan, Do:Shonan, Udenan, Dehya' Hon A:Deyaye

We are blessed with the world, our land,
with seeds, and with precious gifts.

Good Living Since Time Immemorial

Since time immemorial, each tribal community has had examples of its members living upright, good, and pure lives. Stories about what they have done get passed on to every generation. In each telling, we are encouraged to hear the stories. If the storytellers are still alive, we are reminded to observe and learn from them. Together, as a community, we remember the truths and behaviors that teach us to live in a good way.

What does an upright community do every morning? How do they wake up? How do they set their intentions for the day? How do their mouths speak and how do their bodies move throughout the day? And as the sun sets, how do they trust and prepare for the next? What are the activities that motivate them toward peace and good living among one another?

I remember waking up every morning to pray outside with my family. We faced the east, the direction in which the sun welcomes all of creation and ushers in the day. Psalm 74:16 speaks of our Creator, "The day is yours, and yours also the night; you established the sun and moon." I was taught to acknowledge that the Creator holds the setting and rising of the sun and the moon, that our relation to that fact helps guide our intentions as we integrate our ways of living into the rhythm of its seasons. Through this morning ritual, I was taught to give my prayers in gratitude and to ask for blessings for my family, my people, the rest of creation, the universe, and myself.

I was reminded of my humble limitations, that there is no need to overtake or gain for myself more than what is needed for the day.

Peaceful people have descendants. Our origin stories have reminded us to do as much as we can to live peacefully where we are today. We have been taught to continue in the way of prayer. And though we know that all cultures have the stain of mistakes and brokenness, we listen and live out the sacredness of living in a good way and continue in that path. So, I continue on the path of my ancestors, and I teach my daughters the same. I continue to go outside to pray. I pray with them, saying, "Creator, you govern our days with the rising and the setting of the sun and moon. Our ways are in your hands. Teach us now to join in the rhythm of your creation. In gratefulness, we ask for your blessing and for the blessings of the rest of creation—universe, friends, and family."

No matter where I am, I tell the story of my people as I live out my identity. It comes with careful responsibility, and I cherish it. In Zuni, one of the greatest compliments that you can get is being described to others as *dewułash ho'i.* It is a compliment that travels well. To be a friendly, cheerful person means that I can engage with others in kindness. It means that I have the heart to be welcoming and considerate to different groups and households. It means that I embody the motivation to respectfully work and speak in a way that generously values everyone I meet.

I embrace and continue to carry on the values of my community: *hon delanko'ha:willi:wa* ("We will be empathetic with one another"), *hon i:yayyułashik'yana:wa* ("We will respect one another"), and *hon ko'hoł lewuna:wediyahnan, wan hon i:tse'manna* ("We will think before we act and consider how the consequences of our actions will affect others"). These are just a few of our core values that demonstrate how to live as an upright Zuni person. I pay attention to the signs.

There is a definite future implication or consequence in the two paths that Psalm 37 describes. One describes a future, a following of generations. In an Indigenous community like Zuni, this is a cherished inheritance. Having generations follow and participate in what was from the beginning is a sweet blessing. To say, "This is the way we have existed from time immemorial" is upright living. So, I notice goodness when I see my village organize itself to relate in generous reciprocity. I notice goodness when we greet one another cheerfully. I notice goodness when we consider each other in kind regard and peaceful existence. The other path implies a cutoff to future generations. No more existence. How frightening!

One time or another, each community, society, group, or family has asked itself, "Which way is the best way to go? How then shall we live?" The psalm gives us an example of how a group learned to ask itself these questions. *What is a good way to live? What is a not-so-good way to live? What questions do your people, your community, or your family ask to assuredly live in the good way that our Creator instilled in us? What are the words that your people use to describe a life that is trustworthy, faithful, and good? What kind of values promise its people that there will be generations to come after it?*

Oh, good people of God, how gracious God is to offer us help to live a righteous and good life. How gracious he is to provide good examples of individuals, people groups, and communities to teach us the ways of old. I am young, yet I offer myself as a humble teacher from the Zuni people. May it be that you would see yourself and your ancestors as good, being gifted by the values and ways that have guided descendants by the Spirit. Remember that you are the living goodness of the Spirit's delight. As my people are not an individualistic but rather a collective community, I have offered you a historic look at our good ways. "Whether you turn to the right or to the left, [my prayer is that] your ears will hear [God's] voice behind you, saying, 'This is the [good] way; walk in it'" (Isa. 30:21).

TWENTY-NINE

A Mighty Strong Tower

The salvation of the righteous comes from the LORD;
  he is their stronghold in time of trouble.
The LORD helps them and delivers them;
  he delivers them from the wicked and saves them,
  because they take refuge in him.

Psalm 37:39–40

K. A. Ellis is the director of the Edmiston Center for the Study of the Bible and Ethnicity. She is an African American woman who is passionate about theology, human rights, and Christian endurance. She collaborates with the Swiss-based organization International Christian Response as they serve and equip the persevering church. Her research explores Christian endurance from society's margins.

Who among us doesn't want to feel safe?
Our need for safety is hardwired from our garden days (Gen. 1:28–31). Full, God-given shalom in our hearts—relational peace, provision, purpose, and the presence of God—is so ingrained that we long for it for ourselves and those we love. The world God spoke into existence and the people he fashioned with his hands were all created for this kind of shalom.

Yet, the fallen world in which we live leaves us with insecurities that only the presence of the Creator of the original "peaceful world" can fully satisfy (see Gen. 3). For those who have mostly experienced a measure of safety and comfort, it's difficult—even foreign—to understand the sheer physical terror and toll of feeling unsafe, unprotected, vulnerable, or hunted; some of us have never mouthed the silent scream or lost control at the hands of cruelty.

And so, after meditating on the instability of this fallen world, in these two short and final verses the psalmist points us to the Strongest Tower of all: the Unconquerable Great Citadel, with the greatest Sentry of all (see Pss. 32:7–8; 121:1–4; 127:1; Isa. 27:3), inhabited by the King of all creation. The psalmist declares that the climax of the psalm is the climax of this life: the *only* Fortress that can hide our very fragile souls, constructed by, for, and of the only indestructible force:

> Christ, the Progenitor of Peace and Protection, our solid
> and immovable Rock.

Safe from Others in the Nasty Now

Life, with its many jagged edges, can be dangerous. The psalmists and the teachers of Proverbs continually give us the only prescription for desperate times:

> The name of the LORD is a fortified tower;
> the righteous run to it and are safe. (Prov. 18:10)

Lamine[1] is learning this psalm "by blood." He's a citizen of a country that grew hostile toward Christianity and a Christ follower who watched rising oppression and persecution around him. Lamine and his family fled their home country for a neighboring country to be safe, but they soon realized they had moved from frying pan to fire as the government's military apparatus followed and persecuted them there. Upon fleeing back to their home country, their livelihood was destroyed, their family harassed, and their every move surveilled.

As each earthly fortress they chose crumbled, Lamine and his family called out to the Strong Tower to guide them via underground to God's people. Even as bullets and traitors littered their path with obstacles, they found themselves covered by the Great Sentry himself as he moved them through minefields of injustices. So it is with all of God's own.

Though healing takes time in the Strong Tower after navigating such a traumatic, shalom-shattered world, our bodies and minds can find rest with Christ and know the peace for which we were originally created. It is possible after such trauma to once again sleep peacefully like a baby at a mother's breast. When the enemy of our souls has obliterated *all* the safe places and we still *must* flee, there is power in the name of Jesus.

Safe from Ourselves in Eternity

When God acts, it is always full, whole, and complete. The Strong Tower doesn't provide merely earthly physical protection; the psalmist also takes us into the spiritual realm—the redemption and protection of our souls. Like Christ, who created before him and who was incarnated after him, the psalmist addresses both sides of injustice—earthly and cosmic.

You see, the wiser aunties and uncles who came before us understood the complex nature of sin, that "but for the grace of God," the oppressed live on the razor's edge of wickedness themselves. Being delivered from tyranny is no guarantee that we will not ourselves become tyrants.

From the moment our parents rebelled in cosmic treason against their Creator in the garden, they needed a Strong Tower not only for their bodies but also for their eternal souls. He promised to protect his people from eternal damnation through Christ's life, death, resurrection, and glory—a shield around us, the glory and lifter of our heads (Ps. 3:3–4) who delivers us from the false shame wrought by injustices done against us, and the shame of our own cosmic treason committed against him.

> Being delivered from tyranny is no guarantee that we will not ourselves become tyrants.

Unless we enter the Strong Tower of cosmic justice, we aren't truly safe. Yes, he will save us from destroying others; yes, he will save others from destroying us. But Someone must also save us from destroying ourselves! Someone must ransom our souls back to the presence of the One who made us!

The psalmist declares this Someone as the "King of glory, the LORD, strong and mighty . . . in battle" (Ps. 24:8). Christ has accomplished all of this in his finished work on the cross. There is no safe space apart from him.

Once the righteous are in Christ, the Immovable makes himself movable for our complete and utter protection. His presence goes before, behind, above, and under those clothed in Christ's righteousness, an impenetrable soul-fortress with a permanent bond—nothing shall separate us from him (Rom. 8:35–39). Even if our physical lives are lost to an earthly enemy, we will be satisfied to see the redemption of that loss for his glory and our good.

Oh, beloved, when the world's systems fail us, when people fail us, when families reject us, when those who despise Christ revile us, do like the psalmist and call out—call out to the powerful, all-encompassing, movable yet immovable, never-failing name of Jesus:

Salvation!
Stronghold!
Help!
Refuge!

Run straight through the loving gates of the Strong Tower—and be safe on all fronts.

Eternal and just God, the old song describes you as "so high they can't get over you; so wide they can't get around you; so low they can't get under you; they must come in by and through the Lamb— Jesus Christ."[2] Father, I want to come in and find safety and rest for body and soul. Guide my enemies also to you, and bring us all to love and trust your finished work on the cross. Amen.

Althea Brown Edmiston (1874–1937)

Wife, Mother, Intrepid Missionary, Educator, Linguist

Beautifully brown and brilliant, she laid down her life for
the Kingdom; she laid it all down for God's people;
she laid it all down for her King.

Althea Brown Edmiston saw the psalmist's juxtaposition between righteousness and wickedness with her own eyes: first, as the daughter of emancipated slaves who built a new life for her family, and then as a missionary bringing the gospel of physical and spiritual freedom to numerous people groups in the Congo Free State.

As one of the earliest graduates of the historically Black Fisk University in Nashville, Tennessee, Althea Brown was well prepared to have a biblical response to the injustice she saw at home and abroad.

In 1904, Althea married her devoted missionary husband, Alonzo Edmiston, a graduate of Stillman College (also an HBCU[3]). The two were commissioned by the Presbyterian Church to serve in Africa's Congo Free State and served under the leadership of William Shepherd, being discipled by extraordinary missionary saints like Maria Fearing (Mama Wa Mputu).

As the Edmistons ministered, they experienced persecution for their faith from their surrounding culture—from the traffickers of the Arab slave trade and also from King Leopold, who debased the Congolese people under the horrific rubber trade. They were well acquainted with the protection afforded by the powerful name of Christ, often their only defense against hostile cultural forces bent on destruction and dehumanization.

At the same time, Mrs. Edmiston witnessed incredible spiritual transformation among the thousands they served through discipleship and spiritual formation.

The Edmistons believed that through our union with Christ, the people of God around the world and throughout history are practically and spiritually connected, whether thousands of miles away or in one's own backyard. As part of the twentieth century's first African American missions team, they endured hostility to establish faith-work projects and day schools. Althea is credited with developing the first written grammar for the local language, translating Scripture, schoolbooks, hymns, and more.

Althea served faithfully in Congo until she succumbed to sleeping sickness and malaria in 1937. Alonzo continued his global vision and local focus until his death in Alabama in 1954. When Jesus called them each home, they entered the presence of the great Strong Tower himself—the peace, provision, and shalom of their eternal home and King—where no destructive or invasive thing can ever dwell.

Now, you women, hear the word of the Lord;
open your ears to the words of his mouth.
Teach your daughters how to wail;
teach one another a lament.

Jeremiah 9:20

THIRTY

What Carries Us Home

A Poem for Generation Z

Medgina Saint-Elien (Haitian American), **Tasha Jun** (Korean American), **Grace P. Cho** (Korean American), **Mazaré** (African American), and **Mariah Humphries** (Mvskoke Nation citizen)

My mother taught me the way to tie my shoes: a GPS
    on walking upright,
Laces tangled like the drama of Mrs. McMiller asking if
    Haiti was an imaginary friend.
My mother tightens peace to my feet each morning; I
    stumble in the dark.
A kiss goodbye, a burden of how-to's and what not to
    do's in my backpack,
A keychain of forget-me-nots on my wrist, the verse of
    the day glows from my tablet.
In my palm, immortal hashtags stack notifications; on
    my tongue, Creole melodies loop a map back home.

I float forward fast and sure-footed,
My insides warm from spicy soondubu jjigae[1] slurped
    from a circle spoon.
The warmth propels me onward like fire, and my arms
    move like a seesaw, ahead and back again,

Until I come to a spot where the sidewalk tilts; I tilt too.
A car slows and the driver rolls his window down and
shouts, "Go back to where you came from!"
I look back to where I came from, but home is hard to see.

The words reverberate in my soul, growing louder with their
echoes.
They sway and shift the foundations of what I know to be
true, making me doubt my safety, my belonging;
The streets I know so well become a foreign land, though I
am not a foreigner.
Clutching the fragments of myself, I remember my mother
standing at the door,
An immigrant who's walked these streets before, and her
words
Straighten my back and guide me home to where I came
from:

Brave one, remember. As you reach the neighbor's rosebush,
lioness stance.
Watch for those silhouettes of stranger things—
The kind who strike necks and reach for keys in *sankofa*
flowerpots.
Remember the duck and glide.
The shriek from way down underneath that scatters silence
and says,
"Vile ones, you will surrender to our God, who hears our
song and delivers us home."

The corner light replaces the sleeping sun as I watch my
daughter emerge from the waking darkness.
Illumination dances with her movements; the shadows wait
their turn.
I taught her our ancestors' melody, but darkness hums its
own tune.

Younger ones need my attention. I release the Pendleton
blanket from my shoulders and go inside,
My ears in tune with the familiar refrain getting stronger as
she gets closer; my breath still holds.
I breathe out as the matriarchal echoes whisper, *We are*
singing with her. She knows the way.

My key waltzes into the lock; wafts of steam whistle from
the rice cooker and bless my homecoming.
I drop my bags on the floor, and the absence of tension
unsnaps the scrunchie in my hair.
Jamaican castor oil travels down the map of my scalp: the
trace of wisdom as my portion.
Hands clean from what I've carried, a fire of news blaze like
a telenovela.
A quick commercial break unclenches my fists.
Blood rushes back to my fingertips and sends the text to my
temple, *I'm home.*

*From the editor: This book has been an intentional intergenerational
effort. As the editor of this project, I wanted our writing community of
spiritual mothers, aunties, grandmothers, sisters, and friends to invite
Generation Z to reflect on their wilderness experience—an unprecedented
time of a global pandemic; political and economic uncertainty; increased
racialized violence and domestic terrorism in the United States; and the
ongoing oppression, inequity, and abuse against women. We shared our
Psalm 37 devotions with them, and they offered their cries of injustice,
their sadness, and their hopes with us. Our poets then collaborated to
capture the sentiments of their fears and anxieties, alongside the comforts, wisdom, and steady teachings that have guided us along the way.*

*To our girls: We are with you,
every single one of you. We are
here to stand watch; to pray;
to affirm your humanity—your
girlness, your womanness, your
ethnicity, and your culture.
We are here to care, and to
comfort, and to teach you how
to persevere until we all find
our way home.*

EPILOGUE

Living Up to a Name

"Itunu"—that's the name my driver and faithful companion, Michael, gave me. He spoke it slowly, softly, sweetly again, "Itunu," before his lips parted to reveal his Kodak smile and the beautiful white teeth etched across his dark brown skin. I was nearing the end of my trip in Lagos, Nigeria, having led a women's mentoring conference and teaching Bible studies, a leadership and ethics class, and several mentoring workshops. I had also listened to the stories and testimonies from the persecuted church in the area. I was exhausted and experiencing mixed emotions because I longed for home, and I also loved the people so much; I knew that I would especially miss the women. Michael said that the women wanted to give me a Nigerian name, and specifically that Miriam from the theological campus insisted that it must be a good one.

"Itunu," he said. "It's a wonderful name. It's the name of somebody who wipes away your sorrow." He went on to explain that when a family is praying and waiting for a baby for a long time, some for as many as thirty years, they will name the arriving child Itunu once

Epilogue

God answers the mother's prayers. For God had "put an end to her sorrow." Apparently, that is who Miriam said that I was to her.

I have carried this name with me for a few years, and while I was writing this project, editing the drafts, offering the prayers, and clarifying the vision, this name kept returning to me. So, I reached out to our Nigerian poet, Ifueko, to ask if she could provide me with more information about this name.

She reminded me that Nigeria has over four hundred languages. English is the official language "thanks to colonialism"; however, the three major Nigerian languages are Hausa, Igbo, and Yoruba. *Itunu* is a Yoruba name that means "comfort" or "to soothe the mind." She reinforced that the name is given to a child born after a period of disaster or bereavement in a family, who considers the arrival of the child as a comfort to their sorrows. She also revealed that the name, given in its longer form, *Itunuoluwa*, means "the comfort of God," *Oluwa* being "God" in Yoruba. Therefore, I have been encouraged as I draw this collection to a close to remind us of the comforting work of God, the Holy Spirit. In this present darkness and through all of our wailings, we can declare:

> Praise be to the God and Father of our Lord Jesus Christ, the Father of compassion and the God of all comfort, who comforts us in all our troubles, so that we can comfort those in any trouble with the comfort we ourselves receive from God. (2 Cor. 1:3–4)

I pray healing and comfort over all you wailing women, and especially over the ones who have shared the gifts of themselves and the stories of their people with us in this book. May we never shame them, blame them, ignore them, or take them for granted. I thank them for trusting me as their midwife to deliver this gift to you, and for giving me the opportunity to again look up to the God who comforts and embrace the essence of my name.

BENEDICTION

God of our weary years,

God of our silent tears,

Thou who has brought us thus far on the way;

Thou who has by Thy might

Led us into the light

Keep us forever in the path, we pray.[1]

Selah.

ABOUT THE CONTRIBUTORS

Bethany Rivera Molinar is a *fronteriza* Chicana living and working in El Paso, Texas. She is the executive director of Ciudad Nueva Community Outreach and serves on the board of the Christian Community Development Association. Bethany is passionate about faith-based community development and worshiping God with mind, body, and spirit. Instagram: @bethanyriveramolinar

Carolina Hinojosa-Cisneros is a Tejana, Chicana, and *Mujerista* writer and poet from San Antonio, Texas. She is a member of the board of directors for Arts, Religion, Culture (ARC). In her work, Carolina explores storytelling, faith, and social justice. cisneroscafe.wixsite.com/carolina

Dennae Pierre is the executive director of the Surge Network and co-director of City to City North America. She serves at Roosevelt Community Church, a multiethnic church in downtown Phoenix. Dennae is Latina and grew up in a mixed-culture home that introduced her to the importance of bridging cultures.

Grace P. Cho is a Korean American writer, poet, speaker, and the editorial manager at (in)courage. She creates space for people to be known, nurtured, and challenged through her work and desires to elevate Women of Color's voices in the publishing industry. gracepcho.com; Instagram: @gracepcho

Ifueko Fex Ogbomo, alias Lady InspiroLogos, is a self-employed Nigerian writer, poet, performing artist, author, and sickle cell activist. For her internationally acclaimed work in the performing arts, she was classified as an "Alien of Extraordinary Ability" and awarded United States permanent residency in 2017. She enjoys sharing the gospel through storytelling. ifuekoogbomo.com; Instagram and Twitter: @inspirologos

Jenny Yang is the senior vice president of Advocacy and Policy at World Relief, where she provides oversight for all advocacy initiatives and policy positions for the organization and leads the organization's public relations efforts. She is a Korean American leader who has worked over a decade in refugee protection, immigration policy, and human rights. Jenny is coauthor of *Welcoming the Stranger* and a contributing author to three other books. Twitter: @JennyYangWR

K. A. Ellis is the director of the Edmiston Center for the Study of the Bible and Ethnicity. She is an African American woman who is passionate about theology, human rights, and Christian endurance. She collaborates with the Swiss-based organization International Christian Response as they serve and equip the persevering church. Her research explores Christian endurance from society's margins. karenangelaellis.com

Kat Armas is a Cuban American writer and podcaster from Miami, Florida. She is the author of *Abuelita Faith: What Women in the Margins Teach Us about Wisdom, Persistence, and Strength* and the host of *The Protagonistas* podcast. Her work sits at the intersection of race, ethnicity, gender, spirituality, and Scripture. katarmas.com

Ka Richards is the wife of African American pastor Jahill, the mother of five, and a grandmother. As a Hmong American daughter of refugees, she grew up in impoverished multiethnic communities. She currently ministers in a predominately African American context, is a Charles Simeon Trust instructor, and is a contributor to the book *His Testimonies, My Heritage: Women of Color on the Word of God*.

Kathy Khang is a Korean American writer, speaker, and yoga teacher based in the north suburbs of Chicago. She is the author of *Raise Your Voice: Why We Stay Silent and How to Speak Up* and serves on the board of Christians for Social Action. KathyKhang.com

Kristie Anyabwile is an African American author and editor of *His Testimonies, My Heritage: Women of Color on the Word of God*. She is the associate director of women's workshops at the Charles Simeon Trust and a founding member of the Pelican Project. She disciples women at Anacostia River Church in Washington, DC, where her husband is senior pastor. They have three children. kristieanyabwile.com

Lisa Rodriguez-Watson is the national director of Missio Alliance. She also serves as the associate pastor of discipleship and equipping at Christ City Church. A proud Cuban American, Lisa is an activist for immigration reform. She is a writer and conference speaker. Lisa lives in Washington, DC, with her husband and three kids. Instagram: @lrodwatson

Mariah Humphries (MTS) is a Mvskoke Nation citizen, writer, and educator. Through her experience navigating the tension between Native and white American culture, she brings Native awareness to non-Native spaces. With over twenty years of vocational ministry service, she is focused on theology, racial literacy, and reconciliation within the American church. Mariah Humphries.com; Instagram and Twitter: @MariahHumphries

Marlena Graves (MDiv) is a Puerto Rican writer, adjunct professor, and PhD student living in the Toledo, Ohio, area. She has worked with migrant farm workers, asylum seekers, rural and urban poor, and in pastoral roles. She is a bylined writer for numerous venues. Her book *The Way Up Is Down: Becoming Yourself by Forgetting Yourself* won *Christianity Today*'s 2021 Spiritual Formation Award of Merit. marlenagraves.com

Mazaré is an African American spoken-word poet who describes herself as raw honey, "a teaspoon of brutal truth fresh from the comb—bold and thick with sweet." She is the community life coordinator at Grace Downtown in Washington, DC. Experience her poetry album, *Raw Honey*, and more at Mazare.net. Instagram and Twitter: @MissPoeticMaz

Medgina Saint-Elien is a writer and creative who is called to highlight the elephant in the room throughout her work. This Haitian American poet is a Fulbright Scholar and an emerging voice of direction in the media industry. She redefines beauty at Byrdie Beauty, Snapchat, and beyond to amplify the stories of Women of Color. Instagram: @itsmedgina

Michelle Ami Reyes is an Indian American author, speaker, and writer. She is the vice president of the Asian American Christian Collaborative (AACC) and the co-executive director of Pax. She is also the scholar-in-residence at Hope Community Church in Austin, Texas, where her husband, Aaron, serves as lead pastor. She is the author of *Becoming All Things: How Small Changes Lead to Lasting Connections Across Cultures.* michelleamireyes.com

Natasha Sistrunk Robinson is the president of T3 Leadership Solutions, Inc., and the visionary founder of the 501(c)(3) nonprofit Leadership LINKS, Inc. This African American woman from South Carolina is an author, host of *A Sojourner's Truth* podcast, speaker, consultant, and coach who engages, equips, and empowers people to live and lead on purpose. NatashaSRobinson.com

Noemi Chavez has served as the lead pastor at Revive Church, a multisite in the greater Los Angeles area, for over fifteen years. She is the daughter of Mexican immigrants. Noemi is the cofounder of Brave Global, a nonprofit bridging collaboration of church and state to better serve girls on probation and in foster care. Noemi also serves as chair of the board for Exponential Español, a church-planting network. lifeatrevive.com; braveglobal.org

Patricia Raybon is an award-winning Colorado author, essayist, and novelist who writes stories of faith and mystery. Her debut 1920s mystery novel, *All That Is Secret: An Annalee Spain Mystery*, was a *Parade* magazine fall 2021 "Mysteries We Love" selection and a PBS *Masterpiece*'s "Best Mystery Books of 2021: As Recommended by Bestselling Authors." As an African American follower of Christ, she encourages people globally to love God and each other. patriciaraybon.com

QuaWanna N. Bannarbie is an African American writer and teacher who was born and raised in historic Americus, Georgia. She contributes weekly to the *Suffolk News-Herald*, the newspaper of Suffolk, Virginia. She is a founding director for the nonprofit Leadership LINKS, Inc., and instructs at Indiana Wesleyan University. She and her husband, Tyrone, have three children. QuawannaNBannarbie.com; Instagram: @beingquawanna

Rebecca Deng is the author of *What They Meant for Evil: How a Lost Girl of Sudan Found Healing, Peace, and Purpose in the Midst of Suffering* and one of the eighty-nine Lost Girls of Sudan who came to the US in 2000 as unaccompanied refugee minors after living eight years in the Kakuma Refugee Camp in northern Kenya. She is an international speaker and advocate for women and children victimized by war. She is African American of South Sudanese origin. facebook.com/RebeccaDengMedia; Twitter: @rivkadeng

Renee Kylestewa Begay is from the Pueblo of Zuni, located in the southwestern part of New Mexico. She is married to her high school sweetheart, Donnie Begay, and they have three daughters. She is the national director for Nations, a conference speaker, and manages a resource website called The Talking Circle. She founded the Nations movement—a national ministry that seeks to build relationships with the Native American community. thetalkingcircle.com; Instagram: @reneebegay

Ruth Buffalo is a citizen of the Mandan, Hidatsa, and Arikara Nation and originally from Mandaree, North Dakota. She is married to Brian, and they have two sons and two daughters. She is an educator, public health professional, and politician. Ruth was recently elected to the North Dakota legislature representing District 27 in a four-year term as a state house representative. She is a women's peacemaker fellow and founder of Local Innovative Leadership Initiative. Instagram: @ruth_anna_buffalo

Sandra Maria Van Opstal, daughter of Colombian and Argentine immigrants, is the founder of Chasing Justice. She is an author, pastor, and activist reimagining the intersection of faith and justice. Her work centers contemplative activism under the mentorship of the global church, for the mobilizing of the next generation of leaders. She holds a master of divinity from Trinity Evangelical Divinity School. Her most recent books include *The Next Worship: Glorifying God in a Diverse World* and *Forty Days on Being an Enneagram Eight*. chasingjustice.com

Sheila Wise Rowe (MEd) is a truth-teller and is passionate about faith, emotional and racial trauma healing, and (re)conciliation. She advocates for the dignity and rights of the marginalized and abused. For thirty years Sheila was a therapist in Boston, France, and South Africa, and is now a sought-after writer, speaker, and spiritual director. She authored *Healing Racial Trauma* and *Young, Gifted, and Black: A Journey of Lament and Celebration*. SheilaWiseRowe.com

Tarah-Lynn Saint-Elien is a multi-hyphenated millennial who inspires women through her *Cosmopolitan UK* nominated brand, Adorned in Armor, and *Dressed for Battle* podcast. The *Teen Vogue* It Girl turned fashion writer was crowned Miss Black New Jersey and earned her master's from Syracuse University. The Haitian American beauty queen is the author of *Claim Your Crown* and *Love Letters from the King* and has been featured on CBN, the *Haitian Times*, and the YouVersion Bible app. tarahlynnadorned.com; Instagram and YouTube: @iamtarahlynn

Tasha Jun is a Korean American writer, storyteller, and poet. She grew up in a multicultural, biracial family in cities all over the world. She is married with three kids. She writes about faith, ethnic identity, belonging, family, and finding beauty and shalom. Her work has appeared in numerous online and print publications, devotionals, and Bible studies. tashajun.com

Vivian Mabuni is a Chinese American speaker, author, Bible teacher, and host of the *Someday is Here* podcast for AAPI (Asian American Pacific Islander) women. She is the author of *Warrior in Pink: A Story of Cancer, Community, and the God Who Comforts* and *Open Hands, Willing Heart: Discover the Joy of Saying Yes to God*. Viv and her husband, Darrin, have served more than thirty years in vocational Christian ministry. They are proud parents of three young adult kids. vivianmabuni.com; Instagram: @vivmabuni

NOTES

Foreword

1. "Jesus Is a Rock in a Weary Land," traditional African American spiritual.

Introduction: Answering the Call to Lead in the Dark

1. McClatchy, "Girlfriend Live Streams on Facebook after Philando Castile Shot by Officer in Minnesota," *Kansas City Star*, February 7, 2018, https://www.kansascity.com/news/local/crime/article103161887.html.

2. "Heartbreaking Video Shows 4-Year-Old Scared After Seeing Philando Castile Shot," YouTube video, 2:03, posted by *Inside Edition*, June 21, 2017, https://www.youtube.com/watch?v=IHUacoxL1oQ.

3. "Black & Asian Christians United Against Racism," Asian American Christian Collaborative, Facebook Live video, recorded at Apostolic Faith Church Chicago, 2:58:16, https://www.facebook.com/watch/live/?v=798344307462494&ref=watch_permalink.

4. See Matt. 26:6–13; Mark 14:1–9; John 12:1–7.

5. Mark D. Futato, *Interpreting the Psalms: An Exegetical Handbook* (Grand Rapids: Kregel Academic, 2007), 29.

Chapter 2 When the Evil Flourish

1. Latin for "unwelcomed people."

2. Paul Hofmann, "Theresa Named Doctor of Church, First Such Honor for Woman," *New York Times*, September 28, 1970, https://www.nytimes.com/1970/09/28/archives/theresa-named-doctor-of-church-first-such-donor-for-woman.html.

3. Hofmann, "Theresa Named Doctor of Church."

4. Jürgen Moltmann, "Teresa of Avila and Martin Luther: The Turn to the Mysticism of the Cross," *Studies in Religion/Sciences Religieuses* 13, no. 3 (September 1984): 265–78, https://doi.org/10.1177/000842988401300302.

Chapter 3 Blessings in Brokenness

1. French for "praise."
2. The Outpost, "Women Warriors of Haiti and Dessalines the Liberator," WilderUtopia, January 24, 2018, https://www.wilderutopia.com/international /humanity/jean-jacques-dessalines-and-the-women-warriors-who-liberated -haiti/.
3. Marlene Daut, "The 19th Century Kingdom of Hayti Was the Wakanda of the Western Hemisphere," *Quartz*, January 28, 2019, https://qz.com/africa /1535122/the-19th-century-kingdom-of-hayti-was-the-wakanda-of-the-west ern-hemisphere/.
4. Marlene L. Daut, "Why Did *Bridgerton* Erase Haiti?," *Avidly*, January 19, 2021, https://avidly.lareviewofbooks.org/2021/01/19/why-did-bridgerton-erase -haiti/.
5. The Holy Bible was transmitted in this way for centuries before the texts (canonical books) came together as a written collection.
6. Levanjil is the Haitian word for "gospel." *English-Haitian Dictionary*, s.v. "levanjil," https://haitian.english-dictionary.help/english-to-haitian-meaning -gospel.
7. Ledia Bonhomme, interview by Tarah-Lynn Saint-Elien, December 9, 2020.

Chapter 4 Roll Upon the Lord

1. Walter Brueggemann, *The Message of the Psalms: A Theological Commentary* (Minneapolis: Augsburg, 1984), 9.
2. Francis Brown, *The Brown-Driver-Briggs Hebrew and English Lexicon: with an Appendix Containing the Biblical Aramaic: Coded with the Numbering System from Strong's Exhaustive Concordance of the Bible* (Peabody, MA: Hendrickson Publishers, 1996).
3. Spanish for "grandmother."
4. "The Nobel Peace Prize 1979," The Nobel Prize, accessed December 20, 2020, https://www.nobelprize.org/prizes/peace/1979/summary/.
5. Professor John Sanness, Chairman of the Norwegian Nobel Committee, "Award Ceremony Speech," The Nobel Prize, accessed December 20, 2020, https://www.nobelprize.org/prizes/peace/1979/ceremony-speech/.

Chapter 5 Anger, I Will Not Tame Her

1. *Haenyeo* are free-diving "sea women," also known as "Korean mermaids." These female divers from the province of Jeju dive for mollusks, seaweed, and other treasures to provide for themselves and their families. They are a unique Korean sisterhood of women and symbolize such strength. Archana Ram, "Honorary Haenyeo," Patagonia.com, accessed February 5, 2021, https://www.pata gonia.com/stories/honorary-haenyeo/story-86484.html.
2. 엄마, Korean for "mom." 어머니, Korean for "mother."

Chapter 6 My Ancestors' Perseverance, My Voice to Carry

1. Recommended reading: Mark Charles and Soong-Chan Rah, *Unsettling Truths: The Ongoing, Dehumanizing Legacy of the Doctrine of Discovery* (Downers Grove, IL: InterVarsity, 2019); and Steven T. Newcomb, *Pagans in the Promised Land: Decoding the Doctrine of Christian Discovery* (Golden, Colorado: Fulcrum, 2008).

2. This "kill the Indian and save the man" mentality is reflected in the *American Experience* documentary "In the White Man's Image." See "In the White Man's Image," YouTube video, 56:26, posted by "James Starkey," May 10, 2015, https://www.youtube.com/watch?v=RUCIMqlztd0&t=1122s.

3. See articles: Mary Annette Pember, "Death by Civilization: Thousands of Native American Children Were Forced to Attend Boarding Schools Created to Strip Them of Their Culture. My Mother Was One of Them," *The Atlantic*, March 8, 2019, https://www.theatlantic.com/education/archive/2019/03/traumatic-legacy-indian-boarding-schools/584293/. John Yang, "Indigenous Survivor Describes Her 'Haunting Experience' of Boarding School Abuse," *PBS NewsHour*, July 8, 2021, https://www.pbs.org/newshour/amp/show/indigenous-survivor-describes-her-haunting-experience-of-boarding-school-abuse.

4. "Creator, please hear my prayer. I am pitiful. Thank you."

Chapter 7 Pursuing Justice May Start with Anger

1. Elise Hu, "'Comfort Woman' Memorial Statues, a Thorn in Japan's Side, Now Sit on Korean Buses," NPR, November 13, 2017, https://www.npr.org/sections/parallels/2017/11/13/563838610/comfort-woman-memorial-statues-a-thorn-in-japans-side-now-sit-on-korean-buses.

2. *My Wish*, a documentary by Witness and on the website of the Korea Center for Investigative Journalism, 2016. Interview with Kim Hak-sun in July 1997, https://www.youtube.com/watch?v=BAKT6lZPT4E.

3. "Issues Today," Institutionalized Sexual Abuse. See http://www.isajdh.vinlune.com/issues-today.html; and Sol Han and James Griffiths, "Why This Statue of a Young Girl Caused a Diplomatic Incident," CNN, February 10, 2017, https://www.cnn.com/2017/02/05/asia/south-korea-comfort-women-statue/index.html.

Chapter 8 Displacement and Belonging

1. Spanish for "coffee."

2. Fleur S. Houston, *You Shall Love the Stranger as Yourself: The Bible, Refugees, and Asylum* (New York: Routledge, 2015), 99.

3. Shemaryahu Talmon, "Exile and Restoration in the Conceptual World of Ancient Judaism," in *Restoration: Old Testament, Christian and Jewish Perspectives*, ed. James M. Scott (Leiden, Netherlands: Brill, 2001), 110–11.

4. Houston, *You Shall Love the Stranger as Yourself*, 100.

5. Houston, *You Shall Love the Stranger as Yourself*, 107.

6. Houston, *You Shall Love the Stranger as Yourself*, 108.

7. Houston, *You Shall Love the Stranger as Yourself*, 107.

8. Musa W. Dube, *Postcolonial Feminist Interpretation of the Bible* (St. Louis: Chalice, 2014), 147.

Chapter 10 When Will Their Day Come?

1. *Washington Post* Staff, "Donald Trump Announces a Presidential Bid," *Washington Post*, June 16, 2015, https://www.washingtonpost.com/news/post-politics/wp/2015/06/16/full-text-donald-trump-announces-a-presidential-bid/.

2. Julie Hirschfeld Davis and Michael D. Shear, "How Trump Came to Enforce a Practice of Separating Migrant Families," *New York Times*, June 16, 2018, https://www.nytimes.com/2018/06/16/us/politics/family-separation-trump.html.

3. Michelle Mark, "A Detained Mother Says Immigration Authorities Took Her Infant Daughter from Her While She Was Breastfeeding—Then Handcuffed Her When She Resisted," *Business Insider*, June 14, 2018, https://www.businessinsider.com/infant-took-while-migrant-mother-breastfeeding-zero-tolerance-policy-2018-6.

4. Lauren Villagrana, "Border Patrol Still Holds Migrants Outside at International Bridge as Temperatures Rise," *El Paso Times*, June 11, 2019, https://www.elpasotimes.com/story/news/2019/06/11/border-patrol-still-holds-immigrants-outside-u-s-mexico-bridge/1379338001/.

5. Julián Aguilar, "ICE Dumps Hundreds of Migrants with Nowhere to Go at a Bus Station on Eve of Christmas without Warning Shelters," *Texas Tribune*, December 24, 2018, https://www.texastribune.org/2018/12/24/ice-migrants-release-christmas-eve-el-paso/.

6. Tim Arango, Nicholas Bogel-Burroughs, and Katie Benner, "Minutes Before El Paso Killing, Hate-Filled Manifesto Appears Online," *New York Times*, August 3, 2019, https://www.nytimes.com/2019/08/03/us/patrick-crusius-el-paso-shooter-manifesto.html.

7. Traditional Mexican folk bands who play at communal gatherings, including weddings, funerals, parties, etc. Mariachis play the music of the people.

8. Christopher Brito, "Mariachi Band Performs Powerful Rendition of 'Amor Eterno' at Vigil in El Paso," *CBS News*, August 7, 2019, https://www.cbsnews.com/news/amor-eterno-el-paso-texas-vigil-mariachi-juan-gabriel-rocio-durcal-singing/.

9. Spanish for "close friends."

10. David Dorado Romo, *Ringside Seat to a Revolution: An Underground Cultural History of El Paso and Juarez, 1893–1923* (El Paso: Cinco Puntos Press, 2005), 223–44.

11. David Dorado Romo, "Jan. 28, 1917: The Bath Riots," Zinn Education Project, accessed March 15, 2021, https://www.zinnedproject.org/news/tdih/bath-riots.

12. Romo, "Jan. 28, 1917: The Bath Riots."
13. Zyklon-B is a chemical agent that was used in Auschwitz and in Nazi gas chambers during World War II, https://www.britannica.com/science/nerve -gas. Dichloro-diphenyl-trichloroethane (DDT) is an insecticide that the United States banned in 1972, https://www.cdc.gov/biomonitoring/DDT_FactSheet .html.

Chapter 11 Bending the Bow of Peace

1. "Nelson Mandela International Day 18 July," United Nations, https://www .un.org/en/events/mandeladay/legacy.shtml.
2. World Health Organization, "World Report on Violence and Health: Abstract," 2002, https://www.who.int/violence_injury_prevention/violence /world_report/en/abstract_en.pdf.
3. Gyeong Ju Son, "North Korea through a Young Orphan's Eyes," Lausanne Movement, October 18, 2010, https://www.lausanne.org/content/north-korea -through-young-orphans-eyes.

Chapter 12 Just One Suitcase

1. "The Ursuline Sisters of the Roman Union, Central Province, are members of a worldwide community whose lives and mission are rooted in the Gospel of Jesus and the spirit of their foundress, St. Angela Merici. We are grounded and empowered by our relationships with God and one another, in prayer and community, seeking always to be a compassionate, reconciling presence of God in the world." Ursuline Sisters: Contemplatives in Ministry, Order of St. Ursula Central Province, "We Are Ursuline," accessed March 16, 2021, https://www .osucentral.org/.https://www.osucentral.org/.
2. Teresa Delgado, "In Memoriam: Ada María Isasi-Díaz," *Religious Studies News*, accessed December 10, 2020, http://rsnonline.org/index19fb.html.
3. Ada María Isasi-Díaz, *Mujerista Theology* (Maryknoll, NY: Orbis Books, 1996), 62.
4. Isasi-Díaz, *Mujerista Theology*, 205.

Chapter 14 Walking Blameless in the Dark

1. Michael Masser and Gerry Goffin, "Theme from Mahogony (Do You Know Where You're Going To)," 1973.
2. Toni Morrison, *Beloved* (New York: Alfred A. Knopf, 1987), 88.
3. Morrison, *Beloved*, 88.
4. Morrison, *Beloved*, 88–89.
5. Morrison, *Beloved*, 89.
6. Lev. 19:18; Matt. 22:39; Mark 12:31; Luke 10:27.
7. Chanequa Walker-Barnes, *I Bring the Voices of My People: A Womanist Vision for Racial Reconciliation* (Grand Rapids: Eerdmans, 2019), 10–11.

8. Nell Irvin Painter, ed., *Narrative of Sojourner Truth* (New York: Penguin Books, 1850), 12.

9. Nell Irvin Painter, *Sojourner Truth: A Life, a Symbol* (New York: Norton, 1996), 74.

10. Tupac Amar Shakur, *The Rose That Grew from Concrete* (New York: Pocket Books, 1999).

Chapter 15 The Wicked Will Perish

1. *Buddhist Birth Stories; or, Jataka Tales*, trans. T. W. Rhys Davids (London: Trübner and Company, 1880), 1:38, 317–20.

2. Becky Little, "How the 1982 Murder of Vincent Chin Ignited a Push for Asian American Rights," *History*, May 5, 2020, https://www.history.com/news /vincent-chin-murder-asian-american-rights. See also the 2009 documentary *Vincent Who? The Murder of a Chinese-American Man*.

3. Kelly Wallace, "Forgotten Los Angeles History: The Chinese Massacre of 1871," *Los Angeles Public Library* (blog), May 19, 2017, https://www.lapl.org /collections-resources/blogs/lapl/chinese-massacre-1871#:~:text=The%20 bodies%20of%2017%20Chinese,events%20of%20the%20previous%20night.

4. John Eligon, Alan Blinder, and Nida Najar, "Hate Crime Is Feared as 2 Indian Engineers Are Shot in Kansas," *New York Times*, February 24, 2017, https:// www.nytimes.com/2017/02/24/world/asia/kansas-attack-possible-hate-crime -srinivas-kuchibhotla.html.

5. "Behind 'The Statement on Anti-Asian Racism in the Time of COVID-19,'" YouTube video, 1:08:38, posted by "Asian American Christian Collaborative—AACC," April 1, 2020, https://www.youtube.com/watch?v=HdpEQe -32ew&t=322s.

6. Russell Jeung, "Battling Anti-Asian Hate Is an Expression of God's Kingdom," Asian American Christian Collaborative, October 8, 2020, https://www .asianamericanchristiancollaborative.com/article/battling-anti-asian-hate-is -expression-gods-kingdom.

7. Steve Mullis and Heidi Glenn, "New Site Collects Reports of Racism Against Asian Americans Amid Coronavirus Pandemic," NPR, March 27, 2020, https:// www.npr.org/sections/coronavirus-live-updates/2020/03/27/822187627/new -site-collects-reports-of-anti-asian-american-sentiment-amid-coronavirus -pand.

8. Maranatha is an Aramaic phrase that means "Come, our Lord!"

9. Aisha Khan, "Overlooked No More: Pandita Ramabai, Indian Scholar, Feminist and Educator," *New York Times*, November 14, 2018, https://www.nytimes .com/2018/11/14/obituaries/pandita-ramabai-overlooked.html.

10. Dan Graves, "Pandita Ramabai Reclaimed Rejects," *Christianity*, May 3, 2010, https://www.christianity.com/church/church-history/timeline/1801 -1900/pandita-ramabai-reclaimed-rejects-11630514.html.

11. Graves, "Pandita Ramabai Reclaimed Rejects."

12. Khan, "Overlooked No More."
13. To learn more about the Mukti Mission, visit https://www.mukti mission.us/.

Chapter 16 Generous Like Our God

1. Desmond Tutu, quoted in Brian Rusch, "Striving for Ubuntu," *Nonprofit Professional Performance* 2, no. 3 (September 2015).
2. As promised to Abraham in Genesis 12.
3. These are the same temptations presented to Jesus in Matthew 4:1–10.
4. Erika Lee, *The Making of Asian America* (New York: Simon & Schuster, 2015), 60–61.
5. "Chinese Girl Wants to Vote: Miss Lee Ready to Enter Barnard, to Ride in Suffrage Parade," *New York Tribune*, April 13, 1912.
6. Mabel Ping-Hua Lee's speech titled "The Submerged Half" urged the Chinese community to promote girls' education and women's civic participation. Cathleen D. Cahill, "Mabel Ping-Hua Lee: How Chinese-American Women Helped Shape the Suffrage Movement," National Park Service, https://www.nps.gov/articles/000/mabel-ping-hua-lee-how-chinese-american-women-helped-shape-the-suffrage-movement.htm.
7. Kerri Lee Alexander, "Mabel Ping-Hua Lee," National Women's History Museum, 2020, https://www.womenshistory.org/education-resources/biographies/mabel-ping-hua-lee.

Chapter 17 Este Mvskokvlke, paksvnkc, mucvnettv, pakse

1. National Congress of American Indians Policy Research Center, "Research Policy Update: Violence Against American Indian and Alaska Native Women," February 2018, https://www.ncai.org/policy-research-center/research-data/prc-publications/VAWA_Data_Brief__FINAL_2_1_2018.pdf.

Chapter 18 Though We Stumble

1. Dalton Bennett, Joyce Lee, and Sarah Cahlan, "The Death of George Floyd: What Video and Other Records Show about His Final Minutes," *Seattle Times*, May 30, 2020, https://www.seattletimes.com/nation-world/the-death-of-george-floyd-what-video-and-other-records-show-about-his-final-minutes/.
2. Lonnae O'Neal, "George Floyd's Mother Was Not There, but He Used Her as a Sacred Invocation," *National Geographic*, May 30, 2020, https://www.nationalgeographic.com/history/2020/05/george-floyds-mother-not-there-he-used-her-as-sacred-invocation/.
3. Edgar B. Herwick III, "The 'Doctresses of Medicine': The World's 1st Female Medical School Was Established in Boston," *GBH News*, November 4, 2016,

https://www.wgbh.org/news/2016/11/04/how-we-live/doctresses-medicine
-worlds-1st-female-medical-school-was-established-boston.

4. "Dr. Rebecca Lee Crumpler," Changing the Face of Medicine, U.S. National Library of Medicine, updated June 3, 2015, https://cfmedicine.nlm.nih
.gov/physicians/biography_73.html.

5. Judy Moore, "A Pioneering Woman of Many Firsts," *Charlotte Gazette*, February 19, 2021, https://www.thecharlottegazette.com/2021/02/19/a-pioneer
ing-woman-of-many-firsts/.

6. Herwick, "'Doctresses of Medicine.'"

7. Rebecca Crumpler, MD, *A Book of Medical Discourses: in Two Parts* (Boston: Cashman, Keatings and Co., 1883), https://collections.nlm.nih.gov/book
viewer?PID=nlm:nlmuid-67521160R-bk#page/10/mode/2up.

8. Crumpler, *A Book of Medical Discourses*.

Chapter 19 Hunger Pains

1. Yella Hewings-Martin, PhD, "The Science of Hunger Explained," *Medical News Today*, October 31, 2017, https://www.medicalnewstoday.com/articles
/319921.

2. Christina Regelski, "The Soul of Food: Slavery's Influence on Southern Cuisine," U.S. History Scene, https://ushistoryscene.com/article/slavery-southern
-cuisine/.

3. Paulette Brown-Hinds, "Soul Food," *Black Voice News*, January 1, 2005, https://blackvoicenews.com/2005/01/01/soul-food/.

4. Colonial Williamsburg Foundation, "African Diaspora Culture," Slavery and Remembrance, 2022, http://slaveryandremembrance.org/articles/article
/?id=A0057. Also watch the Netflix original series *High on the Hog: How African American Cuisine Transformed America*.

5. https://www.congress.gov/congressional-record/2015/03/26/extensions
-of-remarks-section/article/E434-3.

6. Samuel Momodu, "The Albany Movement (1961–1962)," BlackPast, August 31, 2016, https://www.blackpast.org/african-american-history/albany
-movement-1961-1962/.

7. Glenn M. Robins, "Americus Movement," *New Georgia Encyclopedia*, July 15, 2020, https://www.georgiaencyclopedia.org/articles/history-archaeology
/americus-movement.

8. Tulani Salahu-Din, "Hidden Herstory: The Leesburg Stockade Girls," National Museum of African American History and Culture, July 12, 2018, https://
nmaahc.si.edu/explore/stories/hidden-herstory-leesburg-stockade-girls.

9. Addie's sister Susan was also in the church at the time of the bombing. She survived the bombing but was permanently blinded. "16th Street Baptist Church Bombing (1963)," National Park Service, last updated November 19, 2020, https://www.nps.gov/articles/16thstreetbaptist.htm.

Chapter 20 The Lord Loves Justice

1. Martin Luther King Jr., "I've Been to the Mountaintop," address delivered at Mason Temple, Memphis, Tennessee, April 3, 1968, https://www.american rhetoric.com/speeches/mlkivebeentothemountaintop.htm.
2. David Miller, "Get Home Safely: 10 Rules of Survival," Salt, June 1, 2020, https://www.saltproject.org/progressive-christian-blog/2015/1/14/get-home -safely-10-rules-of-survival.
3. Harriet Ann Jacobs, *Incidents in the Life of a Slave Girl*, ed. Francis Smith Foster and Nellie Y. McKay (New York: Norton, 2001), 120.
4. Jacobs, *Incidents in the Life of a Slave Girl*, 49.
5. Jacobs, *Incidents in the Life of a Slave Girl*, 97.
6. Jacobs, *Incidents in the Life of a Slave Girl*, 5.

Chapter 22 Meekness, Not Weakness

1. Ginger Thompson and Tim Weiner, "Zapatista Rebels Rally in Mexico City, *New York Times*, March 12, 2001, accessed March 13, 2021, https://www .nytimes.com/2001/03/12/world/zapatista-rebels-rally-in-mexico-city.html.

Chapter 23 A Heart That Speaks Wisdom and Justice

1. "Hmong: Our Secret Army—CBS *60 Minutes*," narrated by Mike Wallace, produced by Barry Lando, *60 Minutes*, CBS, 1975, YouTube video, 16:15, posted by "Yawm Saub," February 21, 2011, https://www.youtube.com/watch?v=iFRgOjG-gvU.
2. "Hmong: Our Secret Army."
3. "Hmong: Our Secret Army."
4. "Special Guerilla Units," Minnesota Remembers Vietnam: The Story Wall, Twin Cities PBS, video, 1:35, 2017, https://www.mnvietnam.org/story/sgu/.
5. "The Hmong and the Secret War," PBS, video, 56:52, aired November 9, 2017, https://www.pbs.org/video/the-hmong-and-the-secret-war-zwwpgu/.
6. SommerFilms, "Hunted Like Animals—Hmong Hunted and Tortured— Merciless," YouTube video, 6:21, last updated January 4, 2008, https://www .youtube.com/playlist?list=PL27D812DE4D247A96.
7. William Lloyd-George, "The CIA's 'Secret War,'" *The Diplomat*, February 25, 2011, https://thediplomat.com/2011/02/the-cias-secret-war/.
8. "Metro Transit Police Investigating after Woman Is Seen Being Kicked in the Face on Light Rail Platform," video, 0:26, *WCCO 4 News at 5*, May 6, 2020, https://cbsloc.al/2WBWvDl.
9. Danielle Wallace, "Texas Man Accused of Stabbing Asian Family over Coronavirus Could Face FBI Hate Crime Charge," *Fox News*, April 2, 2020, https:// www.foxnews.com/us/texas-man-stabbing-asian-family-coronavirus-fbi-hate -crime.
10. CeFaan Kim, "Exclusive: 89-Year-Old Woman Who Was Attacked, Set on Fire in Brooklyn Speaks Out," ABC7NY, July 24, 2020, https://abc7ny.com

/woman-set-on-fire-elderly-attack-89-year-old-attacked-bensonhurst-crime
/6333749/.

11. "Anti-Asian Discrimination in the Age of Covid," *Truth's Table*, audio, 1:16, May 2020, https://open.spotify.com/episode/1NmqcwSCXFPxEhd1zMcL7b.

12. "Black & Asian Christians United Against Racism," Asian American Christian Collaborative, Facebook Live video, 2:58:16, https://www.facebook.com/watch/live/?v=798344307462494&ref=watch_permalink.

13. Jessica Lussenhop, "George Floyd Death: 'The Same Happened to My Son,'" *BBC News*, June 14, 2020, https://www.bbc.com/news/world-us-canada-5302 3703.

14. Lussenhop, "George Floyd Death."

15. To the Black community: Please forgive us, Asian Americans, for our complicity and lack of support and solidarity for the past years of racial injustices, police brutalities, and trauma you've endured.

16. "Interconnected Panel Series—AACC & Be the Bridge," YouTube, 4 videos, last updated June 22, 2020, https://www.youtube.com/playlist?list=PLFO18AngoL MebtKsIwd2kbEhf-hNlk8uu.

17. Kassidy Tarala, "Marny Xiong: Lasting Legacy," *Minnesota Women's Press*, November 25, 2020, https://www.womenspress.com/marny-xiong-lasting-legacy/.

18. Daarel Burnette II, "Marny Xiong, School Board Chair and Social Justice Champion, Dies at 31 of COVID-19," *Education Week*, June 11, 2020, https://www.edweek.org/leadership/marny-xiong-school-board-chair-and-social-justice-champion-dies-at-31-of-covid-19/2020/06.

19. Burnette, "Marny Xiong."

20. Brandt Williams, "Fong Lee's Family Angered by Verdict," *MPRNews*, May 28, 2009, https://www.mprnews.org/story/2009/05/28/fong-lees-family-angered-by-verdict.

21. Burnette, "Marny Xiong."

22. Rilyn Eischens, "Data Show Disparities between Black and White Minnesotans in Education, Income, Criminal Justice Are among the Worst in the Nation," *Minnesota Reformer*, June 8, 2020, https://minnesotareformer.com/2020/06/08/data-show-disparities-between-black-and-white-minnesotas-in-education-income-crimina-justice-are-among-the-worst-in-the-nation/.

23. Burnette, "Marny Xiong."

24. "Statement on Anti-Asian Racism in the Time of COVID-19," Asian American Christian Collaborative, https://www.asianamericanchristiancollaborative.com/read-statement, accessed January 26, 2022.

25. Tarala, "Marny Xiong."

26. Burnette, "Marny Xiong."

27. David Griswold, "Marny Xiong, St. Paul School Board Chairwoman, Dies of COVID-19 at 31," *KARE11 News*, June 7, 2020, updated June 8, 2020, https://www.kare11.com/article/news/health/coronavirus/marny-xiong-st-paul-school-board-chairwoman-dies-of-covid-19-at-31/89-3d1b1da5-9081-4685-95ba-d8fb038d39f6.

Chapter 24 Owning My Heritage as Queen

1. Joshua J. Mark, "The Candaces of Meroe," *World History Encyclopedia*, March 19, 2018, https://www.ancient.eu/The_Candaces_of_Meroe/.
2. Mark, "The Candaces of Meroe."
3. Mark, "The Candaces of Meroe."
4. Mangar Marial Amerdid, "Tribute to the Late SPLM/SPLA Commander Ager Gum: The Heroine of the South Sudanese Liberation Struggle," ChildBride Solidarity Organization, March 18, 2019, https://childbridesolidarity.org/tribute-to-the-late-splm-spla-commander-ager-gum-the-heroine-of-the-liberation-struggle/.
5. Amira Adawe and Hodan Hassan, "Skin-Lightening Products Cost Black and Brown Communities Our Money and Our Health," *Sahan Journal*, March 4, 2021, https://sahanjournal.com/commentary/minnesota-skin-lightening-legislation/.
6. "UN Official Calls DR Congo 'Rape Capital of the World,'" *BBC News*, last updated April 28, 2010, http://news.bbc.co.uk/2/hi/africa/8650112.stm.

Chapter 27 The Tree That Withers

1. Michael Janofsky, "Another Plot Against Tough Sheriff, With a Twist," *New York Times*, May 16, 2002, https://www.nytimes.com/2002/05/16/us/another-plot-against-tough-sheriff-with-a-twist.html.
2. SB 1070 was state legislation passed with the intent of allowing local law enforcement the ability to ask any person to disclose their immigration status based on reasonable suspicion. Immigrant rights advocates believed this law restricted the rights of migrants, forcing them to self-deport or end up in the criminal immigration pipeline. It became the blueprint model for other anti-migrant states to enact similar legislation. State of Arizona Senate, Senate Bill 1070 (2010), https://www.azleg.gov/legtext/49leg/2r/bills/sb1070s.pdf.
3. "Sheriff Joe Arpaio Guilty of Contempt for Ignoring Order to Stop Racial Profiling," *The Guardian*, July 31, 2017, https://www.theguardian.com/us-news/2017/jul/31/joe-arpaio-convicted-contempt-immigration-patrols.
4. John Goldingay, *Psalms Volume 1: Psalms 1–41*, ed. Tremper Longman III (Grand Rapids: Baker Academic, 2006), 532.
5. Nigel Duara, "Arizona's Once-Feared Immigration Law, SB 1070, Loses Most of Its Power in Settlement," *Los Angeles Times*, September 15, 2016; "Arizona Grassroots Activists Protest Anti-Immigrant Measure (SB1070), United States, 2010," Global Nonviolent Action Database, https://nvdatabase.swarthmore.edu/.
6. Spanish for "the Vanguard."
7. Cynthia E. Orozeo, "Garcia, Eva Carrillo de (1883–1979)," Texas State Historical Association Handbook of Texas, https://www.tshaonline.org/handbook/entries/garcia-eva-carrillo-de (published October 1, 1995, accessed February 17, 2022).

8. For more on Eva Carrillo de García, see the Texas State Historical Association biographical entry by Cynthia E. Orozcos and Austin History Center's Collection Inventory, *Alberto Gonzalo and Eva García Papers*.

Chapter 29 A Mighty Strong Tower

1. This name has been changed for security reasons.
2. Traditional African American spiritual, composer(s) unknown.
3. Historically Black College and University.

Chapter 30 What Carries Us Home

1. Soft tofu stew.

Benediction

1. "Lift Every Voice and Sing: The Negro National Anthem," J. Rosamond Johnson and James Weldon Johnson.

CONNECT WITH
NATASHA SISTRUNK ROBINSON

To learn more about Natasha and her work as an international speaker, leadership consultant, and diversity and mentoring coach, follow her online!

—— **NATASHASROBINSON.COM** ——